Shopify

The Definitive Guide to Setting Up Your Store

(Step-by-step Guide for Beginners to Build Your Online Business)

Kirsten Booker

Published By **Jordan Levy**

Kirsten Booker

Shopify: The Definitive Guide to Setting Up Your Store (Step-by-step Guide for Beginners to Build Your Online Business)

ISBN   978-1-77485-745-8

Legal & Disclaimer

The information contained in this ebook is not designed to replace or take the place of any form of medicine or professional medical advice. The information in this ebook has been provided for educational & entertainment purposes only.

The information contained in this book has been compiled from sources deemed reliable, and it is accurate to the best of the Author's knowledge; however, the Author cannot guarantee its accuracy and validity and cannot be held liable for any errors or omissions. Changes are periodically made to this book. You must consult your doctor or get professional medical advice before using any of the suggested remedies, techniques, or information in this book.

Upon using the information contained in this book, you agree to hold harmless the Author from and against any damages, costs, and expenses, including any legal fees potentially resulting from the application of any of the information provided by this guide. This disclaimer applies to any damages or injury caused by the use and application, whether directly or indirectly, of any advice or information presented, whether for breach of contract, tort, negligence, personal injury, criminal intent, or under any other cause of action.

You agree to accept all risks of using the information presented inside this book. You need to consult a professional medical practitioner in order to ensure you are both able and healthy enough to participate in this program.

TABLE OF CONTENTS

Introduction

The most straightforward way to establish an online store for yourself is to use Shopify. Shopify is an all-inclusive eCommerce solution for businesses who are looking to sell their items on the internet. Therefore, you don't require huge amounts of capital or investment to get your business started. All you need is a great idea and an efficient Internet connection. Additionally, you don't require any expertise in technology to design an online shop. If the idea of creating a website is intimidating, don't fret because you're not all alone. A lot of people are like this until they realize how easy Shopify is. Shopify makes your job easier and takes just 20 minutes to build the foundation for your online store with Shopify. Shopify is an amazing and user-friendly platform that permits you to personalize your online store, sell whatever products you like and accept various types of payment, while also providing excellent customer service.

If you're looking for easy setup and a hassle-free shopping cart that allows you to focus on the core tasks of your business choose

Shopify. In this guide, you'll discover the secret to creating and running a successful online business selling products using Shopify. No matter if you are an individual or a medium-sized business, or are beginning to think about an online store, Shopify offers a variety of advantages and features. It is now ready to be used as an online store platform. It was designed specifically for those who aren't proficient in web design and development. Shopify basically makes the whole online store creation process an extremely effortless experience while still maintaining the features you'd like from an experienced e-commerce platform.

The book you'll be taught about Shopify and the advantages it provides, and the best way to create an e-commerce store that will be successful. It is possible that the Shopify store you create could be built on the drop-shipping model and private labeling. After you have carefully read the entire information within this guide, you'll be confident in starting your own online shop on Shopify.

Are you keen to find out more about this? If so, it's time to get started now.

Chapter 1: What Exactly Is Shopify?

A Brief Introduction:

In the beginning, Tobias (CEO of Shopify) was intrigued by the idea of the idea of creating a platform to aid in selling his boards online to an buyer.

Lutke and his business partner Scott mostly focused on creating an online platform that was extremely adaptable and user-friendly. Shopify was first launched in the year 2006 and after that there was no turning back. After a struggle for two years, the creators came together to form a new team that would transform Shopify into the digital platform that we have come to are familiar with and love to this day. The year 2008 was the first time Shopify made its debut revenue and then slowly became aware of itself as an excellent e-commerce platform. Shopify has been able to obtain additional funding of $7 millions in 2010, and 15 million in funding starting in 2011. The humble platform that was founded with the concept of selling snowboards online became a massive online marketplace with more than 500,000 online stores. Shopify is an e-commerce platform that lets store owners create their own online stores. With Shopify you do not have to be concerned about problems with server maintenance hosting, branding, or hosting for customers. The many tools that are available are easily accessible within Shopify and will assist in addressing each of these issues.

Shopify provides many options for customization that range from inventory management to monitoring of customer usage, online store management, and even customer contact. The principal purpose is the primary goal of Shopify is to assist prospective entrepreneurs, as well as online store owners to set up their own eCommerce stores even if they do not have the necessary technical skills or programming experience. The features Shopify offer are not just flexible, but also extremely simple to utilize. Even if you have no technical expertise you are able to easily start your own online shop to sell items made by other people or your own creations. The many challenges involved in the creation and launch of an eCommerce company are solved through the use of Shopify as an hosting platform.

Based on this short history the process of starting an online store is a challenge and carries some risk. The reason that the majority of people are successful in this lucrative venture is because reaching the point at which your business is successful requires a lot of commitment and not much luck. Shopify's mission is to assist more people who are looking for a job in e-commerce achieve their goals with help and less risk. Although creating your own eCommerce website is definitely some effort, Shopify is there to simplify the process than beginning with a blank slate.

It achieves this by providing an outline to work from when you create your site. It's like a template permitting you to create an online store for your business without having to learn the intricate web design process or spending money on experts to apply the skills you need. Shopify provides a variety of essential tools that are pre-designed and ready to use in your store including themes for your website to be designed around, as well as shipping and transaction options, and the ability to translate your site so that you can sell your products in many countries without worrying of the language barrier. It's an extremely useful platform that can provide the advantages of having a store on the internet for more than skilled and experienced web developers.

Who is using Shopify?

Shopify is utilized by thousands of companies and has more than 2 million clients. There are a myriad of products available and unique to every company and makes Shopify an outstanding competitor to some of the best e-commerce platforms available.

What is Shopify? Shopify Function?

Shopify's platform is split into two segments:

"The frontend. This is the section that customers see which is the face that Shopify (which also includes your online store) which customers view and browse on their own.

Backend. This is the area which only the store owners are able to view, and which is where you create your website and can make updates and changes to the user's experience as needed. This is where you'll add new products, alter your design, and apply specific individualization and customizing to suit your requirements (such for social media hyperlinks).

With Shopify's platform, you can promote the items you choose to sell. Once you're prepared you'll be able organize your items so that buyers can locate them by dimensions, styles, colors and more. With ease. Shopify has built-in transaction gateways, allowing you to decide on the price you want and watch buyers arrive to buy your items on the internet. Shopify's user-friendly software lets you have the idea of a new product grow from an idea to being launched and ready to sell to customers in a matter of hours.

What is it that makes Shopify So Effective?

As I mentioned earlier, creating your own website for e-commerce is a difficult process. Shopify is a great tool to help ecommerce owners to achieve their goals while avoiding risk and difficulties. It lets you get straight to the point and earn money while avoiding tiny (but essential) steps that are only possible through platforms like Shopify instead of attempting to build your own, starting from scratch. Here are some instances of the benefits Shopify offers those who want to become e-store owners.

Web Design

Making a website is a lot of work, not just in regards to aesthetics and theme, but also the coding process and maintenance in general also. If you build a site by yourself, even if that you aren't an experienced web designer, you'll need to employ a professional prior to moving on to an enviable business. It could cost you an enormous amount in terms of profits particularly when you're yet to earn any revenue from your business.

The process of creating a website with Shopify is easy since the coding, themes and even maintenance are completed before you begin to build your shop. Instead of creating the design on your own You can choose from a range of pre-made choices and then customize your website to meet your specific needs from there.

Option for Transactions

Similar to integrating the payment method into your website requires a qualified programmer to install it securely. This means ensuring the security of the system since it is the money of your customers and financial security that we're talking about, as well as developing other essential functions like shipping calculators which are difficult and if not a painstaking task.

Another time, Shopify already has these features covered and can be easily integrated on your site with just a couple of clicks.

Fulfilling Orders

Delivering orders from customers requires more than just cardboard boxes that have addresses on them as well as stamps and mailers. This is more than your own personal efforts or the small group you can manage on their own.

Shopify handles the issues like creating official shipping labels and other tasks such as working with the

Dropshipper will be less difficult as compared to trying to manage a separate website on your own.

The Small Details

Shopify handles every one of the minor, but important, duties that you'd need to take care of throughout your career should you decide to launch your own website. This is exactly what Shopify does.

Shopify's mission is making sure you take care of little things to allow you to cut short to the chase that is, focusing on your company and its products as well as your clients.

Chapter 2: How To Set Up A Shopify Store

Here, we'll take a closer look at the steps you need to follow to establish an online store on Shopify.

Step 1. Signing Up

The first step in the process of creating an Shopify online shop is signing to Shopify. To sign up, visit Shopify's Official Shopify website and fill out the signup form in order to establish an account. Make sure to click the "start free trial" button once you've entered all the necessary information. Be aware that the store name you select for must be distinctive, or Shopify will ask you to select a different name. Once you've entered your mail address you'll have to provide a few of additional personal information like your name, name, country address, email address, telephone number and alternate email address and the list goes on. Additionally, you'll be asked to answer questions regarding the items you want to sell, if you already have those products and the items you wish to sell. If you're just browsing through Shopify to get a better understanding of how it operates, select the "I'm simply playing with it" option from the drop-down menu, "Do you have products?" Choose "I don't know," in the section which asks "What are you selling?" When you are content with your responses and you have completed all required fields, click "I finished" to finish the signup procedure.

Step 2: Log In

After you've completed the signup process you have the option of logging out , or go on. If you're not logged in then log back in and navigate to the screen for the store administrator. When you arrive at the store admin screen, it's time to personalize the store add products, upload them, and configure different types of shipping and payment.

Step 3. Configuration

Let's look at the various settings you must set up when configuring the store. Here are the steps to follow when setting up the store to meet your needs.

Choose the Settings menu, then select general options.

There are several general data points that you can modify or update for example, the store's details such as standards and formats such as store currency, the address of your store. The store's details include the other information you could need to include is an email address that will be used to get any assistance from Shopify and the store's name as well as a customer's email address that prospective customers will receive whenever they get an email sent from the store. Be sure to include the official name for your company, the address of the street as well as a contact number. There are a variety of formats and standards to select from. You should carefully choose the unit system and the weight unit that is default and also the appropriate time zone. Beyond that you must select the correct store currency. Based on the country in which you operation, the currency used by the store will be different.

Select PowerSettings Payment providers

The setting of the payment method or payment method is vitally important. First step setting your Shopify payments. Then, you need to activate the third-party payment service. It is also possible to activate a second payment method or alternative method for payment. In addition do not forget to activate the manual payment option too. Make sure that your payment authorization settings are safe and simple to remember.

Settings Shipping

The name suggests that on this page of the menu of settings, you can change or add details about shipping origin and shipping rates, the weight and size of your packages, or allow third-party fulfillment services. The shipping source is the name of the place used to calculate your overall shipping cost. Based on the location of shipping and the associated shipping rates, you are able to specify specific rates for shipping when you check out. When calculating the cost of shipping be sure to take into account the weight and size of the package to be delivered.

Settings Checkout

A crucial aspect of an effective e-commerce site includes the check-out page. When you are on the page for checkout, you are able to make modifications to the customer's account, contact with the customer orders, order processing email promotions, check-out the language and other policies of your online store. When you create a customer account you are able to select whether a buyer needs to create an account before they can check out or not. Contact with customers basically offers the option to choose whether customers are required to provide a particular phone number or email address prior to completing their checkout. Additionally, it gives you the option of choosing any other method that the customer are able to use to receive delivery notifications. Customer forms let you choose whether you wish to collect additional details from customers before they complete their purchase or not.

When processing an order, various information about your checkout procedure, including the information provided on the page for checkout, the order delivery, the billing address along with the delivery address will be included. In order to promote email marketing, you could give customers to sign up or join your marketing emails. Make sure you check the language used on your checkout pages. Beyond that there are different rules and regulations, and you'll need to complete the checkout page with specifics including the refund policy, the conditions of service, as well as the privacy policies.

Settings Notifications

This page provides a variety of notification options, including delivery notifications, notification to the customer and notification of orders. Customer notifications pertain to all transactions processed by your online store including information regarding invoices, order cancellations, confirmations of orders, refunds for orders as well as abandoned carts. The various shipping notifications comprise delivery update, fulfillment request and delivery or shipment shipping confirmation, shipment, and delivery confirmations for shipping. You have the ability to choose the type of notification you'd like to receive or do not want to receive. Once all the notifications systems are set up, it will help to ensure that your company is in the right direction.

Taxes and Settings

If you do not wish to be in any legal troubles, you need to ensure that your shop has all the required permissions and pays all taxes in time. Based on the current tax policies of the country or state that the store is situated in, tax rates may differ.

Settings Sales

Controlling the sales channel is essential for every owner of an e-commerce store. With this feature you are able to easily manage sales channels or add them to your current e-commerce store. Sales channels allow you sell online via social media, mobile devices, or in person.

Settings Files

Make use of this feature to upload images, videos or other files. You can also control all documents you upload by using this option.

Settings Billings

The name implies the section deals with all billing related with the Shopify store. The billing information contains information on all invoices paid by one of the payment options available on the site. It is also possible to add credit card details to pay for other invoices on the platform. To get a complete overview of all fees and the payouts including the Shopify subscriptions, or the shipping costs make sure you check the invoices and fees option.

Settings Account

On this page there are all the necessary information in order to control you Shopify account. It offers an overview of the account as well as the status of your account, as well as what Shopify plan you selected. If you have additional employee accounts linked to the primary Shopify account, then you should use the permissions and accounts options to manage your other accounts. You can also pause your store, shut down it, close the Shopify Store, or engage an expert through Store status.

4. Adding Products

Go to the dashboard, select products, click on the button to add new products. Within this area, you'll have the option to create new goods for your store to sell them right away. To start you need to click on"add product" and then click on the "add item" button and then provide the necessary product's title as well as any additional information that is associated to the product. There are two ways to upload products. You can either manually add items or import them in bulk. To add products manually you'll need to provide details for every item, such as description of the product titles, images categories prices, variants, and other details. It is also possible to bulk import all of the items by importing them through CSV (comma separated values) file.

If you do not have a product then you can select a duplicate option. After you have duplicated the item, you are able to alter the design as you receive new products. However, if you're looking to add any variation to a particular product make sure to click the "add different" button.

Step 5 5. Assigning the products

It is now time to assign the various items to collections. To accomplish this, select the option for products from the menu of navigation, go to collections then select the to create collections. Once you've made and added all of the items, it's time to group them into collections. Different collections can help improve the appearance of your products on the menus in your online store.

Two ways through which you can add items in collections to Your Shopify website. The first involves adding the items you'd like to various collections manually. The alternative is to add them automatically. If you choose the automated method, certain products will automatically be added to a particular collection whenever they meet the predefined requirements defined by you.

Step 6 Application of Themes

It's now time to incorporate themes into the Shopify store. First, start the dashboard and then open the online store. Select option settings and choose themes. You can choose themes from the Shopify Theme Store is easy to use and you can begin immediately. There are many themes, both paid and free to pick from on Shopify. Each theme available that is available on Shopify includes an initial preview. You can view the design before you decide to incorporate it into your store. If you decide to go with one of the themes the only thing you have to do is to publish it to your Shopify store. The details about the various themes in the following chapters.

Customization

Modifying the navigation bar is also an essential element of setting up the navigation bar for your Shopify store. First, you must open your Shopify store, navigate to the sales channel section and then click on online store. Choose for navigation. From the menu, click the menu option to add the links you wish to include. In this area you can put in multiple navigational links users will be able to use to browse your store online. You can include hyperlinks for your "About us" page, the policy page as well as your "contact us" page. Consider all the various pages you want to put on the Shopify website and then put the links for them on the menu bar.

Step 8 Pages

There is no way to create any website that does not have pages. After you've included all the required links and you are ready to make the pages that correspond to these links as well. In order to create pages you must open the dashboard, and then click the online store and then select pages. There are a variety of pages your site should have for example, the "about us,"" "contact information,"" FAQs and policies pages. Make sure that these pages contain all the information a prospective buyer might require prior to purchasing from your online store.

Step 9 9. Blogs

You can also include blog posts or blog categories like news about e-commerce to your site. By adding valuable content to your website, you're adding value to potential customers. If your visitors know that they can benefit from visiting your site, the likelihood of them visiting your site will rise. This is also a fantastic method to keep your clients while increasing loyalty.

Step 10 Step 10: Customizing Themes

In the earlier step, you were required to select a theme to use for you Shopify store. Once you've selected the theme, it's time to alter it to give your shop a appear more appealing. When you customize, you're obliged to upload the logo of your store, as well as upload slides of product images , or offers to create an image carousel for your home page. Additionally, you can add related items functionality for every product page. With customization, you're required to select the quantity of items that will appear on every line of collection pages. The selection of the item's placement and the way they are displayed is vital as it affects the overall appearance of the site.

Step 11 Step 11: Domain

Shopify will automatically display the domain name you have chosen for the online shop you have created. Domain names are an online address of your online store. So, it is essential to be able to have a domain. The domain name must be appealing and easy to remember. Shopify will automatically show your domain name on your e-commerce site free of cost. If you wish to test this option for free or buy a custom domain name. If the domain you select is registered, you will be required to modify to a different domain.

Step 12 Step 12: Store Preferences

To view the preferences for your store first, visit the dashboard, then click the option to shop online then click on preference from the. Be sure to look through the various categories available in the store preferences. The various categories must be considered for include Google analytics titles and Meta descriptions as well as password protection Facebook pixel and checkout security. The titles and Meta description will ensure that your online store has been optimized to be found by search engines. By adding Meta information to these description, it permits web crawlers to search and find your website and increase the visibility of your website. When you turn on Google Analytics, you can keep track of all customers who come to your website. Additionally, it generates reports on various metrics and data that you can utilize to create useful insights in the pursuit of more effective marketing strategies. When your store is ready to launch you can uncheck the password in order for your shop to be accessible. If you are planning or need to start an Facebook advertising campaign, you must enter the Facebook pixels ID to build online advertisements. It can help track the effectiveness of your campaigns, identify new customers and focus the marketing effort. To guard your e-commerce shop on Shopify from abuse or spam Complete this Google reCAPTCHA option when you are making your purchase.

Step 13 Step 13: Making payment for Shopify

After you've completed these steps, it's time to pick a Shopify plan to begin. There are five plans on Shopify which are listed below.

Shopify Lite

The Shopify Lite costs $9 per month. If you're unfamiliar with Shopify or are looking to give it to test it out, this is the most affordable alternative that is available. Through Shopify Lite, you can present products on your existing website for different people on Facebook and also make use of Shopify to manage the sales of items, even in physical stores. If you already have a website, this feature is a great option.

Basic Shopify

Basic Shopify is priced at $29 per month. It is the least expensive option for those who want to set up your own online store using the platform. Its various benefits include unlimited storage for files and two user accounts and allows you to sell unlimited items, provides customer assistance 24 hours per day, 7 days a week, gives extensive analysis, assists in generating discount codes, and allows for the blog to be used. In addition it also facilitates the creation of orders by hand, provides full access to the e-commerce features and assists in recovering abandoned carts.

Shopify

The Shopify plan Shopify cost $79 per year and offers more advantages over the earlier plans. It allows you to create gift cards, retrieve lost carts with a higher rate, give advanced reports, and decrease the transaction charges. It also lowers charges for credit cards that are incurred through this site. The option of creating gift cards can be useful for any company which wants to boost its visibility in the marketplace. The plan offered by Shopify provides detailed summaries of sales and customer data. It's perfect for anyone who is involved in a large volume of sales online, sells items on gift cards that are available and needs thorough reports.

Advanced Shopify

The Shopify plan Shopify is $299/month. This plan comes with two functions are available as an addition to those that were offered in the prior plans. This plan not only provides advanced reports, but also details about the availability of live shipping. This plan lets you manage all of the Shopify information easily and build reports that can be easily customized. You can choose from a range of metrics and dimensions to design reports that are customized as well as save them to your computer for later review. There is also a range of filters that you can apply to your data to produce particular results you want to examine.

Shopify Plus

The plan offered by Shopify is priced at $2000 per month. It is also the most expensive that is available on Shopify. It's typically designed for large corporations rather than small or medium-sized enterprises. This is a solution for corporate use which provides all the features discussed up to now as well as additional features such as security, order fulfillment and an interface for applications. Do not choose this option unless you are dealing with a significant amount in sales. You also need an advanced integration between your online store and the internal applications, and you have huge funds.

Take a look at these various plans and choose one that is suited to your requirements and wants.

Step 14 Step 14: Installing Applications

With regards to Shopify There are thousand of apps you can choose from. Each of these apps can be seamlessly integrated into your online store. But, it's important to select the best applications. The various apps you could utilize will aid in the promotion of your online store, give you rewards to your customers, handle the logistics of shipping, keep track of the amount of revenue you earn and even track the inventory. Each and every function you could think of for running and maintaining an online store is easily handled through the application. So, make sure you take your time reading through the various applications discussed in the following chapters.

It is all you need to do is follow the various steps in this article to set up your own Shopify store in the shortest amount of time.

Chapter 3: Niche Marketing

The most crucial aspect of the financial success of an e-commerce career is identifying your market niche. A niche market offers one specific item or a smaller selection of similar items that are targeted to a specific set of customers who might be interested in purchasing from a niche market. Although you might think that you're more likely to succeed by having a wide and wide range of products that your customers can choose from, they will most likely offer an edge but you're best by deciding on the market that you would like to market your products to by focusing all your effort around this. In this way, you will be able to establish your brand as an exclusive and important brand to your selected market far more easily than if you be a generic online store which sells anything that is available. Here is some more information about niche marketing and the best way to know your niche.

Selecting an area of interest

Of course, the initial step is to decide on the field you'd like to focus in. For this, you should ask yourself:

* What are your passions in both your personal and professional life? What kind of products would you find pleasure selling or think would be the most profitable option financially?

In the ideal scenario, you'll need to find a compromise according to what you're looking for in business.

Learning to Understand Your Choosen area of interest

If you're not an experienced expert within your field of expertise learn about the subject before you decide to focus your business on selling products on this market. When you've got a good grasp of what you're doing and let the world know how crucial the products you sell in your niche market are.

Prove their worth by displaying a link to your site in articles on products you sell, or creating your own content explaining the reasons why potential buyers should appreciate your offerings.

Contact websites that feature such articles, and you'll be amazed at how many are willing to offer a bit of free (or at the very least, cheap) advertising.

Designing Your Shopify Store

After you've chosen the specialization you'd like to serve and have learn about the market you've chosen It's recommended to work out the specifics of how your business will operate well ahead of actually launching the store. Consider:

* What kind of products are you planning to sell? Will they be digital or tangible products? If, for instance, you have decided to sell books, you can decide selling printed publications which are sent to your customers , or ebooks that are downloaded instantly after making a the payment. You can even combine both!

* How do you plan to arrange payment options? Do you plan to sell your items separately or provide customers with access

to them via subscription? If for example, you run a bookshop, you could offer individual ebooks and/or books, or opt to offer online access to your books via subscription-based arrangements.

What's the store's layout? Do you think it will be appropriate considering the items you sell and the specific market segment you're operating in? You can choose from one of Shopify's collection of pre-designed themes to choose from. Or, if you want to, you can engage an internet designer to create the perfect theme for your website instead.

* How will you complete orders? Are you going to take advantage of Shopify's shipping option or your own method, or employ dropshippers? If you choose to choose the Shopify method, you'll purchase and receive the shipping label (postage included) to utilize to ship packages to your customers. Shopify customers who choose the more expensive packages will save money with this method.

Which payment methods do you be able to offer your customers? Are you going to utilize Shopify's transaction tools or create your own system? Shopify offers several payment options that you can add onto your shopping cart page for example, Paypal.

* How do you obtain the products you're selling? Do you make the items inside your own facility or use an outside company? Be sure that if you choose to purchase items which you later offer to others at a higher price, you'll be able to earn an income from the price that customers are prepared to pay.

Chapter 4: Designing Your Shopify Website

Setting up the configuration of your Shopify store is a straightforward procedure. In comparison to building a site completely from scratch, it's simple. However, it does take time and practice before you really get the hang of it particularly if you're not a pro at the intricate details that go into web-based design. There are many tutorials and manuals that you can read online to aid you. Below are some general tips to guide you with the procedure of the process of setting up your online store.

1. Picking a package. There are many Shopify Packages to chose from that are designed to meet specific requirements and wants of web store creators from all walks of life. If you're just wanting the basics then you can choose packages that range from $9 to $29 per month. (Packages which include an online store begin at $29 price.) If you're looking to enjoy all the benefits that come with it, consider the $179-a-month package. Additionally, there's an array of between package options available when you're in a gray space. The more expensive the plan you

choose, the more benefits you get like a lower rate on processing charges, discounts for shipping labels as well as other features for your shop.

2. Selecting a theme. Shopify offers a range of themes to choose from more than 100 and all are absolutely free! If you're willing to spend an extra amount there is the option of buying premium themes, which will cost you between $80-$180. The premium themes have more features of higher quality. Also, you can take advantage of not using Shopify's themes alternatives completely and employing a designer to develop your own theme.

3. Adding Your Chosen Products. Once you've selected the product category and market you'd like to concentrate on then you can begin adding the products you want to sell into your online store. This is among the most complicated steps as there are numerous complex sub-steps that you may not have considered in advance. In addition to publishing a list of items for customers to view and possibly purchase once your website goes online, but you're organizing the

products according to style, size color, style, and other details that pertain to them to ensure that customers is able to easily locate what they are looking for. Images must be included and text as well as descriptions for each product. The products you sell are the primary and vital aspect of your website therefore it's only natural that the majority of your efforts are devoted to these.

4. The addition of payment options. One of the major drawbacks of conducting the business on the internet is the process of paying for goods isn't the same as cash, checks or changing a credit card hands. Instead, you must offer a variety of payment options to your customers to integrate to your website. With the Shopify platform, you can choose from a variety of payment options, all already installed and ready to use for you to select from including credit and debit cards, and Paypal and a wide range of lesser-known options. Like we said you can also choose the option of shipping your own items by yourself, using a postage stamp provided by Shopify or using dropshippers to do the job for you.

The Shopify features, add-ons and Tools

Shopify provides a variety of tools and features to help you run your business. In addition to the thousands of third-party applications you can utilize that work with or work seamlessly with Shopify However, Shopify offers a few of its own programs and features that make managing your business easier.

* Accounting Software. Accounting is an integral element of running a successful company. Shopify integrates with third-party accounting software such as Quickbooks, Freshbooks and Xero to assist you with this often daunting task. These programs allow you to keep track of vital financial data like your transaction timeline, tax history and other expenses, without having to hire an accountant who is professional.

* Inventory Management. Another important aspect of operating your online store is keeping an inventory of your items. It is essential to make sure you have enough stock for the days that are expected to see a lot of traffic, like around the coming holidays. Also,

you must be able replace any lost or soon to become missing products before customers place an order the item. With Shopify's inventory management system, you can quickly discern which products are most well-known and those that don't sell in the same amount of time, and replenish your stock more or less frequently depending on the product.

• Customer service. Without your customers, you'd not have a business at all. Therefore, you need to provide an efficient customer service. It doesn't matter if it's about an issue on their part or a request for information regarding a package that was shipped by you, it's an excellent idea to create an auto-responders. This is particularly useful after you've seen a rise in number of customers, since it's difficult or even impossible to respond manually to each email from a client of a successful company or to let every client know that the package has been delivered. Even if it's an automated message that your customer receives, it assures them that you're listening to them and working on their issue. If customers require contact with a person, Shopify also offers tools such as live chat, so that you and your team can interact with them directly.

* Social Media Management. In today's competitive market it's difficult to manage a business that is successful without the use of social media. It can be utilized for advertising, communicating with customers or keeping an eye on other businesses on the market, or any mentioned above, having a Facebook page, or other social media alternatives is the right choice. It is recommended to integrate automated posts into the online social media outlet(s). While you may be able to communicate with your customers through social media, as well Automated posts are great to schedule content frequently or at specific times without having to think about when to schedule it yourself or hiring an outside service to handle the job for you. It also frees up time working on the content of a Facebook or blog post to accomplish something else or responding to feedback from customers or managing a different part of your company. There are many choices available to manage social media that are all are free and work with Shopify.

Chapter 5: Earning Money On Shopify

The most lucrative aspect and we can call it that's what every person works. That's right, money. Shopify is a fantastic way to earn money online. This is a brief overview of some ways you can earn money using Shopify.

Start your own shop

It's definitely one of the best ways to earn money through Shopify. The first requirement is to have something you can sell! If you're not the owner of a traditional bricks and mortar-based business it is possible to benefit from Drop Shipping. Here are a few rules for Drop Shipping:

Affiliate Program

If you don't own your own items to sell and aren't keen on drop shipping then you are welcome to join the

Shopify affiliate program that allows you can earn up $358 per client using referrals from your customers. You have two choices to select from:

1. You can earn residual income as Revenue Share to earn your monthly Income

It's simple to earn commissions on all Shopify customers that you refer to them on your site. Commissions could be as high as $35 per month.

2. Earn Commission per Sale of the Client's subscription

The web traffic affects your revenue to a great degree as the promotions that are available on these sites encourage users who conduct online searches to purchase the product and increase sales.

• Promote Shopify's services on your Review Site

If you're not confident working with the affiliate market, you could earn a steady income through running a review site on Shopify. This helps clients to easily find the most effective and trusted products. If your review site has a good position on the search engine results and is a result of this, it will definitely increase the number of customers who visit your site.

Shopify allows sign-ups on your website, thereby helping you earn more revenue. In order to earn this lucrative income, you should have a good presence on your site, which can help to increase conversion rates.

Show your creativity in Shopify Themes

If you're someone with an imaginative inclined You can create custom themes that catch the attention of clients.

* Create an App for Shopify

It requires a good understanding of programming. If you're adept at it, you can develop an app using the aid with the Shopify API and enhance the user experience. Apps can be a fantastic method for your company to become mobile. They allow you to not only see people browsing your products from wherever they go and they'll also be able quickly glance at your website and check if you've published any news.

The benefits of an app are astounding. It is not just a way to ensure that your customers are up to the latest, but ensure that they are informed about any sales and promotions that you'll be offering. The benefits are huge If you know a ways to do it happen.

The advantages of using Shopify to Earn money

The availability in Shopify packages at affordable prices.

There is a 14-day trial free demonstration.

Free Ecommerce setting up option.

Simple to put into place with GET started option that provides an informative forum for getting your site up and running in just a few just a few minutes. It is all you need to do is create a name for your shop, and then add a concise and appealing description that includes contact information for your business and the address of the shop.

Even even if you don't have any products to offer, you can still earn some money using the Shopify affiliate program.

How to Increase Sales through Social Media

Social media has played crucial roles in the growth of sales on the internet today. The majority of people make use of social media for increasing awareness of their products and attracting their attention.

If, for instance, you're interested in selling the iPhone cases, then the most effective method is to purchase it from Ever paying 4$ and then offer it for $10 with an additional $6 in the price you set for your Shopify store.

This is not all, you can also design an discount coupon for 20% off and promote your offer via Facebook, Twitter or Reddit to attract many people to it.

The majority of people love buying products using coupon codes for discounts and all the time, these sales are taking place in large amounts. Not only that, you can also make Facebook store and then sell your products there.

A Shopify store is exciting entry point into the world of digital retail, however you should be aware of any potential obstacles or challenges throughout the process. Like offline retailers Online stores can test your patience as well as challenge your preconceived notions and test the limits of your knowing and adapting to the changing trends and preferences. This is particularly true in the world of online shopping in which your customers are constantly bombarded with a variety of choices.

The most important thing to consider as an owner of a Shopify store owner and store owner, is to keep in the main goals you have set in establishing an e-commerce store. If your goal is to establish an extra source of income or eventually to expand your store online into your main source of income the long-term viability and longevity should be the primary focus of your attention rather than impulsive, quick-thinking poor-planned strategies that could hinder your financial success.

Chapter 6: Build Your Own Online Empire And Succeed In Ecommerce Business With Shopify

Who wouldn't want to have an online empire and operate an amazing e-commerce venture while at home? To achieve your dream Let's begin by understanding how to create your own online store with Shopify.

Set Up Your Online Store

Online shopping or online store is the latest buzzword you'll hear a lot of. This is a great deal from Shopify that offers a 14-day trial for free trial, which can be signed on the main page. You can also click the Free Trial button available on the menu bar. You must provide your email or password, as well as your store's name.

The URL is your store's name. However, if you want to alter it lateron, the site allows the user to alter it. It is always better to create a simple name that reads like you.myshopify.com because choosing multiple words will show the link like your-business-name.myshopify.com. If you do not want to redirect to a URL that is from your own domain, such as store.yourdomain.com to you.myshopify.com and vice versa, you should keep a store's URL or store's name at hand. It is necessary to supply all the essential information like name as well as address and phone number when creating your account with Shopify. After completing these steps you will be taken into the administration dashboard in order to begin creating your online store. Read the 7 step guide to make the process easier.

1. Include your products

Add products to your online store using manually adding them or by bulk uploading using an CSV file, or imports from platforms like Magento as well as eBay. If you sell digital items First, you must install an application to deliver digital products, to add your products with this application. The online manual of Shopify. Provides additional information on selling digital products. If you are selling services that you wish to sell, you should opt for an application like Product Options with which you can tailor your offerings for customers.

Shopify store lets you offer 100 different variations of products, which generally come with options in terms of size as well as color and finish. The site offers the option of adding an item with a range of options. There is no restriction in this regard if it's an actual product. For instance, you can choose three options for your ebook, i.e., just the ebook, the third is an electronic book with additional materials, and the third option that is comprised of everything, and also the ability to access a personal forum for members. The Shopify documentation clearly explains to how to set up your products.

2. Customize your design

It is the next stage adding an individual design by selecting an appropriate theme. The theme you choose can be found that you like from Shopify's Shopify Theme Store, that offers a variety of themes for free as well in paid. If you don't have any plan and just choose a theme, you are able to modify the theme using the template editor or settings editor to modify the code. The most frequent place you'd want to change is the footer, as it is the area where you could provide payments, social networks as well as other information.

There are a few examples of ideas that could be good to begin with. There are a lot of themes to pick from, but these are the most effective to consider right immediately.

3. Choose Your Domain Name

The Shopify online manual contains all of the details related to setting up the customized domain name for your store. Therefore, instead of being compelled to select the domain you.myshopify.com You can choose among the possibilities such as store.yourdomain.com and yourdomain.com.

4. Create tax and shipping charges.

It is your responsibility to add tax along with extra shipping costs to your products and inform Shopify about this. Shopify will display the basic costs, however it will depend on the item you offer and you may have to add additional options.

5. Payrolls to be set up

This is the most important element of the entire process. Shopify Payments accept credit cards for those who reside located in Canada, the USA, Canada, or the UK. This service doesn't require any payment gateways from third parties or merchant accounts. Shopify integrates additional payment processing options, including PayPal, Amazon Payments, and Google Wallet.

6. Settings

Your entire profile must be created with care. The majority of these information are filled in when you follow the procedure step-by-step. But, it does not require the necessary information for the addition of the Google Analytics code as well as store description and the store's name in the section for your profile as the information needed is all required to be entered within the settings general to you.

7. Start Your Store and show it to the world.

Once all the data is completed, and you're set to launch your store online You can then open it to the public. At that point the store is password-protected, it will remain private and you will be able to test it to see that everything is working as it ought to. Be sure to check every aspect before the client notices the flaws.

Picking Apps with Additional Functionality and Features

Shopify offers numerous free and premium applications that can be used to improve your online store. They can be classified as:

Accounting -- Connect the Shopify store to your accounting account. Shopify store to one of the most popular accounting software like QuickBooks, Fresh Books, and Xero.

Customer Service -It benefits both the client as well as the seller to include live chat, contact forms and feedback as well as other features to support customers.

Inventory Management -Systems for managing inventory, when coupled with an online retailer, can simplify the process.

Marketing - This section lets you integrate your search, email as well as social media advertising in the online shop.

Reporting You can look for additional statistics for your online business by using these applications. It can assist you measure sales and conversion rates and customer behaviour.

sales -- The Sales area assists you in increasing sales through the aid of customer reviews, product reviews, loyalty plans, promotions and suggestions from others.

Shipping -- Make the process of shipping your product faster and more efficiently with applications to help manage the process of fulfillment and connect you with the shipping company you prefer.

Social Media . This is a area that you should not miss out on. Keep in touch with clients and connect with them through social media by using these apps.

Tools -- You'll discover tools that will assist you to manage all the necessary features needed to run an online shop successfully.

The most beneficial and most useful feature for customers is that it provides bulk redirects, battling fraud, translators for languages and RSS feeds.

Not sure where and how to start your own online store? You may need to modify the SEO settings on your product pages. And as a bonus you should add an email marketing service to ensure that customers will join your mailing list. The email marketing services typically provide guidance in connecting the Shopify site to their platform.

Social Selling

It's a completely innovative method of selling that is frequently used nowadays. If you're one of the people who is looking to sell products on your blog, there is a solution. Shopify has widgets and plugins to WordPress, Drupal, and Joomla users. You can showcase products on your pages, posts, as well as in the sidebar. If you're creating content that is based on the interests of your customers it will drive more traffic to your website. Another method of keeping your customers updated and interested is to set up an account on Facebook and share interesting content. Shopify offers a range of Facebook integrations that enable you to transform the Facebook site into an online store.

What about Affiliates?

Shopify has a range of applications that let you create your own affiliate program that will keep records of referrals from customers and other supporters. It is possible to do this should you be interested in giving away your profits to others. It will also generate some publicity.

Where Can You Find Out More

If you're someone with desire to know more about eCommerce and be successful in selling your online store, there's no stopping you. It is easy to find informational materials such as e-books tutorials, guides, and even videos to aid you in learning more about Ecommerce University. You can also visit Shopify Wiki in which you can read all the information you need to know about Shopify and the development the store. Shopify also offers a support section where you will find more than 200 articles for troubleshooting. If you do happen to encounter an issue that is new or unusual You can also use forums to search for assistance. Forums typically contain thousands of subjects that are related to e-commerce.

How You Can Get Help

This is the only option that you can use if you are unable to assist yourself in troubleshooting guide. It is always possible to seek assistance from Shopify Experts. This section offers assistance in the setup of your store and design marketing, developers, and photographers that can transform your online store a profitable business.

Chapter 7: Choosing The Right Keyword Shopify

We'll discuss keyword research and how it can be applied to increase the visibility of your business on search engines. We will also discuss the best way to target ads that are paid. The market research will provide the foundation to accomplish these tasks. In addition, you'll be able to understand your target market simply by studying the habits of potential customers.

One of the first things you should conduct is an easy Google search on the kinds of products you'd like to market and look up what results. The search bar on Google will provide you with similar terms to search results in the process and it's prudent to examine these as well. The main reason is provide you with an idea of the kind of content users are viewing in search results for the exact item. It also allows you to compare yourself to your competitors, and also gives you some ideas on how you can enhance the content that is already available to all.

Going even more into consideration, I suggest to write down the words and phrases that are relevant to the types of products you intend to offer as well as the common themes that are associated with your business, and names for your products. I suggest you write this list so that it is easy to duplicate and then paste it later.

The next step is to utilize these words using the Google Keyword Planner. This tool was created to assist you in creating advertisements and bids that are appropriate for these ads via Google Adwords, the advertisement service Google provides and applies to Google's own results for search. It is possible to gather enough information without opening any advertising campaigns to justify your time.

On the Google Keyword Planner, type in the keywords you've got in your mind and it'll bring up a lot of data. The program offers suggestions for keywords that are related as well as information about how frequently these keywords have been used over the course of a month, and an overall idea of how many people pay to display ads that pop in the results when the keywords are typed into a search box or are connected to the website they're displayed on.

The data is useful because of a variety of reasons. It won't provide you with a precise amount of sales or the many consumers are spending on a specific category of goods however it can aid in determining the extent to which a product or market is trending, whether consumers are actively seeking out information or products using these keywords, and how they are competing. Although a high level of competition using Keyword Planner Keyword Planner doesn't mean you can't sell certain products or that you aren't able to compete in an industry but it does mean that consumers will have a tough finding the product through your store's e-commerce site via Google.

It is advisable to record the key phrases and keywords with low competition and moderate to high volume of searches each month. If possible, it's best to include these key phrases into your product's description and titles in a natural way. We'll go over this in detail in the future, but make sure to write them down while you're doing it Keep them in a place you'll be able to locate these later.

If you're not sure about the direction you want for your e-commerce business, a search for keywords could be the perfect starting base. If you are able to discover a niche that has large numbers of searches, but little amount of competition, it indicates that your competition isn't investing a lot of money to promote their items, which makes it much easier should you choose that direction. It also implies that you'll be one of the first results when users type in the phrase or word. Many business owners have used Keyword Planner and similar tools to identify niches that were not explored in the past. despite the exponential growth of ecommerce in the past ten years, it's possible to locate markets that aren't entirely over-saturated.

Another advantage of this kind of keyword study is that it will aid you with naming your shop or your domain name and even products that have keywords that are effective in search engines.

The term Search Engine Optimization (SEO) can be described as an ever-evolving research and application of how to make your site prominent on search engines, specifically Google. It's a complex issue, but some key principles are applicable to any of your content whether it's blog as well as descriptions of products, videos on YouTube and social media, posts on social media or any other source that you use to increase your presence online. Being aware of the fundamentals will ensure that you don't make common mistakes which can harm your search engine rankings. While the most effective approach to SEO is to work with an expert, these suggestions can assist you in starting.

Content is King

In the end, regardless of any suggestions for SEO The most important factor is that you're creating content that is written well and proofread. It should also be 100 100% authentic. Any content that isn't of the highest quality is likely to harm you in some way or another. High-quality content builds trust in your company's name and that trust will eventually lead to your position in the search engines.

If you're not a skilled novelist, it could be necessary to get someone proofread and edit your writing. If you have a friend who could assist, then absolutely ask for their assistance. Offer to repay them using your products, services or even cash. If you don't have any contacts employing a reliable freelancer on websites like Upwork is recommended.

To make sure your original content doesn't get flagged as a plagiarism, make use of CopyScape (or similar plagiarism-checkers) and then examine your content for plagiarism 500 words at each time. This will inform you where else online that the words you've composed already exist in full. Beware of reusing descriptions from manufacturers and pictures due to this reason.

No number of SEO work is worth it in the absence of quality content. That's probably the most crucial aspect you can accomplish.

Implement Keywords

By using this method, you'll be able to construct an extensive list of keywords. You can then sort the most likely ones to be successful to the least important. As a general rule having a high number of searches with low competition is beneficial.

I've recommended the use of keywords in a variety of places in the product description or blog, for example. As a general rule the keyword should not be used more than once in 100 to 200 words. A keyword that is used too many times on one page could make Google's algorithm mark your website as spam.

Don't use keywords in a manner that doesn't flow naturally. Because your content should be high-quality, adding keywords in a way that isn't done correctly will hurt your sales chances even if it is able to improve your rank on Google.

Include the keywords you want to use in your meta data field titles, meta data fields and your domain's name If you can, and in any place you are able to. Even if you only manage it once and only once, it's better to be able to possess it.

Blog posts can be written with your most popular keywords. It's not just an effective way of giving you something to write about, it also assures you're making use of keywords in an organic and intelligent way. Anybody can create a website by using keywords. Only the best writers and clever SEO strategists can create an amazing article about any keyword.

Videos and Images

Videos and images, particularly when they're original can greatly improve your search engine rankings. It's not just a way to integrate your website into Google's Image and Video search features on Google however, it also provides you with a second chance to integrate keywords into the alt-text as well as the video's description.

Chapter 8: The Steps To The Process Of Preparing Your Pricing Strategy

What price should you market your product?

The price is an aspect that defines your item. It's part of the brand and its market positioning, which is its position within the marketplace compared with other similar offerings (competitors).

Price is thus an essential aspect to be considered when creating your business, not just for the purpose of generating profits but also as an aspect that affects the way your product is perceived by potential customers.

Pricing is usually a source of anxiety for new entrepreneurs. Most likely due to the lack of experience and confidence, the act of pricing the launch of a new service or product could make a lot of new business owners anxious.

A lot of entrepreneurs don't know what price to charge and don't know the potential value of the new product. They may also be worried about the reaction of the market. Are they worried that the cost is too expensive? What happens if they post an online message and say, "It certainly wasn't worth the price!"?

However, you must remember the meaning of a businessis being paid for the value you add to a market. There should be no excuse for not being the money you deserve for your contribution to value.

Pricing is (First) A Psychological Concept

If you are keeping your prices low due to doubt about the quality of your item, that will be evident. The cost of a product is often a sign of the product's (perceived) high-quality. If you believe that by selling your product at a cheap price, you'll steer clear of possible complaints and operate within a safe zone but don't believe it.

Before we go into greater specifics, I'd like to tell a short background.

Just a few months ago I was an active participant in the mastermind team of bloggers and entrepreneurs on the web. The first time we met we introduced ourselves all.

One of us was a coach. The man introduced himself, and then explained the work was going on and with a certain confidence:

"Come to me for a session one time, and you'll be in alignment and gain the ability to stay focused on what you're supposed to accomplish in your life. A single session with me will transform how you feel about yourself." Wow. It was so compelling that I wanted to make an appointment as soon as I saw him. His presentation was convincing. Then, we inquired what he charged per hour. I was expecting at least $1,000. He could have offered $1,500 and it might have been a reasonable price. But he stated $250 for an minute of time. What did you think occurred in my head? Do you think I thought "What is a bargain!"?

It's not quite that simple. This made me question his claims and the results that he was promoting. In just one hour with his company, my life could be transformed, and for just $250. It was a bit odd that I felt the price. The "something" is the price of his services. It was just too cheap and the low cost decreased the perceived quality of his services.

Do you understand that pricing is in essence a mental thing?

Does this mean that it's more beneficial to offer your services at a higher cost just to enhance the value? It's not true... however, the price you display must be in line with the value you're offering.

The price of a product is often linked to the status of the buyer. Certain people are always buying the most expensive shoes and watches because they want to show their "social standing" to be displayed through their clothes and accessories.

The strategy you choose to position your product in the marketplace--your product in relation to your competition's --should have an influence on the pricesince it's the primary factor that buyers will look at when evaluating the quality of your product.

Whatever price you're willing to allow your product to be sold for, there needs to be a reason to justify it. Lower prices aren't necessarily negative, provided that you can justify the price. It's the same when you pay a higher rate.

How do you determine the price of your product

What's the goal of your product?

The first thing to consider will be "Why do you offer this service in the first instance?"

Does it refer to:

How do you gain credibility? (Often it is in the process of the publishing of a book or in the creation of blog)

Do you want to increase the number of email subscribers on your site?

How can you generate revenues?

What's the point of your product have any significance? If you intend to generate prospects (email subscribers) that is, you've got an incentive to give your product away, or at a lower cost because the emails themselves offer a significant value. In this scenario the price will not affect the perceived value of your product. It's justified and may even be beneficial, as you'd like to draw as many qualified visitors to join your mailing list as much as is possible.

If you want to build the trust of your customers, then money shouldn't be the primary goal. Don't opt for a cheap or extremely high cost and instead, look for something somewhere in between. However, if you are looking to earn money that is, then you must aim for the highest cost.

What's the capacity to pay for Your Market of Target?

If you've looked about the avatar's (ideal customer's) profile, you'll know its earnings and budget for discretionary spending and the ability to pay for the kind of service you're providing.

What price could your target audience be willing to would be willing to pay for your service?

If your ideal customer is single parents receiving benefit or university students and you're selling a huge movie theater, you have a great chance that these customers is interested, but even if they are is interested in what you have to offer but not able to afford the screen.

Consider: "Can they pay?"

This is an important factor to take into consideration when choosing the right area of interest. In the ideal scenario, you would like to target a market that is able to generate an income that can be used to purchase items that are not essential.

What is the market's reference Price?

What is the cost for similar products available on the marketplace? What is the price of your competitors offering similar items? That's also an indicator. Examine your competition's features and pricing. Check out the qualities of their products against yours. Consider your own position on the market that you'd like to hold. Are you a budget option, an average or a high-end choice?

Pay for your expenses

Which is the fixed price or the amount you pay regardless of the quantity of products you produce? How much are your variables costs or the price per item that you have created?

For instance, if you are writing a book your fixed price will cover the creation the book such as your writing process, cover illustrations as well as editing and proofreading. The variable cost will comprise the distribution and printing fees per book.

If you've chosen to give your product away free, you'll need to be able to cover both your fixed and variable expenses. If the goal of making the product was to earn money it is possible to market it for minimum three times the variable production cost. However when the intention is to bring in leads (subscribers) and leads, then it is not necessary to cover the costs of production as it is seen than an investment.

What is the perceived value of the benefits your customers are likely to receive from using your Product?

How valuable is the outcome that you offer the market you are targeting? What's the perceived value the advantage?

For instance, how much would someone who is looking to shed ten pounds in order to look stunning before summer begin be willing to pay for a program to lose weight? What about a bride who is looking to wear her wedding gown? or a man who wants to reduce his cholesterol levels to prevent health issues that could be imminent?

Your market of choice will be influenced by price based on the necessity of getting over the "pain" and the urgency of it.

What will it take to help your customers over come that "pain"? If you're providing a weight loss program which promises good results in two months, if you follow an exercise program and healthy eating program, what price will the average person wanting to shed weight fast be willing to spend? What price would this same person pay for a straightforward natural product that will give similar outcomes? It's likely to be more than the workout program, since the work required to achieve the results is lower.

The advantages that can be derived through the use of the product as well as the effort required to use it should be taken into consideration when selecting the product's cost.

The Mattress Method Mattress Method

Marie Forleo, business coach and an entrepreneur, has a fantastic method to describe the value of an item by using the Mattress Method. Are you able to transform its value to the real world currency of money, time and love?

She provides an example of her day when she went out looking for a new mattress. What she was considering is more costly than the other models available However, the salesman informed her that:

You'll be spending about one-third of your day in the bed

A good night's sleep can improve your performance, health and looks

In essence, the salesperson advised her that a good night's sleep made her wealthier and healthier as well as prettier. They are tangible advantages that the item offers in the real world currency. What do you think is the value that your customers will get from the benefits customers get from buying your product?

A Portfolio of Your Products

You must offer a variety of services or products.

For instance, if you offer an eBook at $19 and an online course for $79 and a 1-hour consultation for $250, you've got three items. Offering different levels of product will give people a price-reference to make a comparison.

In the case above in the example above, if you sell an ebook and an online course the online course could be seen by the consumer as being too costly, however adding a higher-priced item, such as the $250 consultation this makes the middle option appear less expensive. It's psychological. The majority of people choose the middle alternative.

Another reason to look into an array of products could be surprising: some customers prefer the highest-end choice. If you don't provide an option that is high-end or higher-priced product, they'll buy another.

The book, 80/20 Sales and Marketing Perry Marshall explains that there always will be those who are willing to purchase a high-priced deal. Marshall gives an illustration of Starbucks. Starbucks sells normal filter coffee at $2.50. There is also an entire breakfast package for $12. This includes a biscotti, soy latte and fruit salad. But have you seen the espresso machine is also on sale? Naturally, all people will be able to afford the espresso maker, however some will. If Starbucks did not have any espresso machines, then the person who was looking to purchase one would purchase it from another place.

Starbucks might lose a sale by not providing the item.

Do you have a premium product you can offer? If not, could you develop one? Not only does offering one will make your other cheaper products appear more reasonable to customers But not offering one is likely to result in a loss of the potential for sales.

The most important thing is to provide a variety of services or products. It assists people in making a an informed purchase when they are able to compare pricing and features.

Discounts Can Be Risky

In general, it's recommended to not offer discounts.

Discounted prices can be extremely addictive. When your product is being sold at a reduced price and are unable to resist, they'll have a difficult to purchase it at normal price in the future. They could be expecting more discounts, but they'll have to wait before making a purchase.

In addition, discounts can cause confusion about the perceived value of your product that you're selling. If it's offered for sale at a lower price is that it's worth less than you offered it for?

The issue is: What do you instead do?

The best approach is to provide additional value in a time-bound period. When it comes to an event, this could be done by adding an additional element to the offer in the form of an additional benefit.

For instance, if you're offering an online course in outdoor photography, you might provide a free ebook about how to capture stunning sunset and sunrise photos for the first 10 purchasers.

If your book is published and you want to offer an audio version with no additional cost, but only for a certain quantity of copies or for a short period of time.

It's a bargain that will benefit your customers without reducing the value of your primary product or inducing customers to reduced costs. Be aware that the bonus product must be related to the primary product and, in the ideal case should be a complement to it.

If You Really Want to Give an Offer of Discount

In this instance, make certain to justify the discount. Provide a reason as to why you're giving the discount.

Are you offering clearance? Are you celebrating your company's 10th anniversary and you'll be happy to offer a discount in order to mark the occasion? Are you offering an exclusive discount offer to your loyal customers to say thank you?

No matter what the cause, make sure you mention the reason. Make sure that people know that this discount is for a celebration to ensure they don't get frequent discounts in the near future.

All-inclusive resorts located near the tropics have discounted rates during the winter months in the northern hemisphere since fewer tourists purchasing their holiday products during this time. That's justified. There's a reason for them to reduce the cost, because the season is low, which means lower occupancy. They could even do better if they upgraded their offering. Instead of reducing the cost of a hotel room or offering food vouchers or free trips in low-season.

Don't be concerned about people complaining about the price of your product.

RamitSethi who is the creator of I Will Teach You To Be Rich, has been repeatedly asked to speak about pricing on various live and podcast shows, like"The Smart Passive Income Show or Chase Jarvis Live.

He confessed to having difficulties charging for his services initially. He was worried about the reaction of his customers even though his first product was only a five-dollar ebook! Yes, some members of his audience were unhappy.

"How are you going to charge us for content? !"

Ramit has been providing important information, free of charge for the past two years prior to launching his eBook for $5.

So, what can this tell us? It teaches us it is inevitable that we'll have people who complain!

Luckily, complainers typically make up a small portion of the audience and aren't the type of audience you'd like to serve. They're not your ideal client. The audience members of Ramit's who complained about the price of the eBook even though they had consumed two years of free content, were not worthy of his attention.

The fact is, it's inevitable to have people who are unhappy who are unhappy, and that's ok. Accept that fact, and stop setting a price for your product.

However, if the complaints you're receiving in relation to the price of your product are generalized, then perhaps you've done something wrong. If so, pay attention to the constructive feedback, and should you be able to, amend the price accordingly.

What Should You Remember About Pricing?

1. Pricing is a part of positioning and branding.

2. Pricing is a very personal thing:

3. It's usually associated with quality.

4. It could also be linked to the status of the person.

5. To determine the price of your product There are a few factors to be considered:

6. The goal of your product

7. The potential for paying of the market you want to target (niche)

8. The market's benchmark cost (other similar options that are available in the marketplace)

9. The perceived value or benefit your product offers

10. It is better to provide different levels of product in order to offer the option of

offering products of various value and at various price.

11. Instead of discounting your item instead, you can offer bonuses for a specific number of transactions or at a specific time period to provide value. In this way, it doesn't decrease the worth of the deal, and you'll keep your customers from being accustomed to discounts.

Chapter 9: The Comparative Analysis Of Shopify To Other Platforms For Ecommerce

If you're studying this text, it's obvious that you're considering Shopify as the platform to host your online shop. The book isn't just intended to educate you about running an efficient e-commerce store however, it is designed to educate you on the advantages from Shopify over other platforms for ecommerce. To provide you with an accurate and balanced review, we'll go over several of the best platforms the world, and also every one of their benefits and disadvantages in comparison to Shopify.

What exactly does what is an Ecommerce Platform?

Ecommerce platforms are program that can provide templates for the creation of an online store. It eliminates the majority of difficult tasks involved in creating a website from scratch such as writing code and managing the intricate aspects of creating the website. It is your responsibility to personalize everything to your preferences by picking from a wide range of templates that are already made and free of bugs.

Stacking Shopify against Other Ecommerce Platforms

Shopify is by far the most used e-commerce platform available in the midst of thousands, perhaps hundreds of thousands of competing platforms. However, it doesn't suggest that it's the best. We'll be comparing Shopify against the other three platforms which include Magento, BigCommerce and Volusion -each of which is joined by Shopify as one of the top five platforms available in the market. We'll concentrate on eight key aspects: pricing and design customization features security, marketing reports, add-ons, and support at the end, you'll have an educated and impartial conclusion about which is the most effective platform.

Pricing. In terms of cost, Magento is the cheapest since it's completely absolutely free, unless you decide to buy it's Enterprise Edition, which is quite expensive. BigCommerce has the highest price of the three, since it comes with four different packages, similar to what Shopify offers, however the cost per month for each package is around double that of Shopify's. In addition, the prices of Volusion are identical to Shopify's.

Design Customization. For each platform, customized designs can be made available through many themes. Certain themes are free while others cost the price of. BigCommerce does not charge any fees for its themes, however the quality of these themes isn't great. Volusion also, as usual is similar to Shopify in cost of themes and quality. It provides a few dozen themes at no cost and more premium themes with a quality that is similar to Shopify's. Magento also offers a range of themes for free, however the premium themes are expensive and costly. Shopify and Volusion maintain the most optimal balance between cost and quality.

Frontend Features. All of these platforms are extremely similar when it comes to features for the frontend. One platform in the group that may be less than the others is BigCommerce due to its lack of organization. But, it makes the up-side by offering more features than the other three platforms including Shopify.

Backend Features. Contrary to the frontend there's nothing missing from BigCommerce in terms of the backend. BigCommerce offers a wide range of options for customization, and simple interfaces that let you design your store to look and feel just like your personal. Shopify is the second option, having an easy-to-use user interface. Volusion and Magento come with backends that are difficult to wrap your brain around and require some time to become familiar with.

Security. This is the area in which Shopify rises to the top as the best platform. Shopify's hosting is top-quality and has the content Delivery Network (CDN) and is PCI compatible. BigCommerce is second in that it's an extremely secure host, but it doesn't have an CDN. Volusion offers hosting as well as an CDN and PCI conformity, however you will need to pay for the encryption Shopify provides at no cost. If you're using Magento, you'll have to buy hosting outside of the platform and pay more out of pocket, however since the base version of the platform is free of any money, it sort of makes up for it.

* Marketing. Marketing is not only about advertising, but also includes SEO, social media as well as other aspects. As always, BigCommerce delivers the best quality since the platform's amazing customisation capabilities extend to SEO optimization. Magento is second-best offering everything you need to use SEO already built in and ready to go. Shopify provides only basic SEO capabilities, and Volusion provides much less. Both platforms appear to be equal with regard to social media integration is concerned. with the exception of Magento and BigCommerce, which don't have the feature. Volusion and Magento have a newsletter service, and Shopify and BigCommerce provide the option to integrate third-party services.

* Promotions. Each platform has same kinds of promotions. Each platform also offers an advertising tool to help to increase visitors.

* Reports. Each platform is identical for this particular category.

* Add-ons. All four platforms have an add-on that gives users the ability to use more features than you initially were able to use. Each platform comes with an app store that you can browse through and download from. It's hard to decide the most suitable platform in this kind of category as apps change constantly and it is difficult to compare the different platforms against one another when they don't stay the same.

* Support. With Shopify you're guaranteed all-hours support regardless of the package. BigCommerce provides support 24 hours a day during the week and select hours on weekends and also an education centre for builders of e-commerce. Volusion provides support via live chat, phone and email 24 hours a day,

Magento isn't supported properly unless you purchase the expensive upgrade for the package. In the absence of that it is possible to visit the forums on the site for assistance and advice.

Chapter 10: Sourcing Suppliers

Before you begin to search for suppliers, we appreciate your business and do not wish for you to be cheated. It is crucial to differentiate between legitimate wholesalers and those that claim to be such. We have already distinguished the two, as well as the terms you can return to the top of the page to refresh your memory of the distinctions. There are also sellers who claim to be wholesalers however they are not. Wholesalers that are legitimate purchase directly from producers and can offer significantly lower prices than retailers.

Here's How to Find Fake Wholesalers:

However, genuine wholesalers seldom invest in marketing, and are typically very well-hidden. That means that when you locate an authentic wholesaler, the chances are that you'll encounter several fake ones. Beware of middlemen who scam you But luckily you are in good hands with us and we are here for you.

They'll ask for annual fees: Have ever had to pay a fee in order to be considered for the job you want? If so you've probably realized that you were cheated. It's the same for these 'wholesalers. They'll ask for an ongoing fee each month to allow an opportunity to work with them. Two words, RED FLAG! True suppliers will never demand you to pay for fees that are ongoing.

But, you must differentiate between directories and suppliers. We'll review directories later however, they're more likely to request for a specific cost, however, theirs will be legitimate and reasonable.

The wholesaler is open to the public. Wholesalers are not able to sell directly to the public. If this wholesaler does, then they are merely a fake retailer who is deceiving the public by offering their inflated prices. But, you must be a registered company and have an account with a wholesaler. Also, you must be approved prior to begin your purchase.

Here are a few of the fees that you'll be charged:

For each order you place: Most drop shippers charge the customer a fee per order you place. The cost will likely be between two to five dollars. It's an issue of how complex and the size of the goods which are being shipped drop-shipped. It is important to note that you aren't being swindled, this is a normal procedure in this business.

A minimum purchase: Wholesalers always require a minimum purchase amount. This is to ensure that they can get rid of people who visit their stores and become annoying and have smaller orders that don't be able to translate into significant business.

If you're using dropping shipping, drop shipping will bring the same issues. What do you do should do if a company requires a minimum order of six hundred dollars, and your company's average order is around two hundred dollars? In this situation the best choice is to make a prepayment to the supplier 6100 dollars. This will allow you to establish credit through these suppliers.

Identifying the Suppliers

If you have the understanding to the real people and those who are not, it's now time to locate some suppliers. Do everything you can in your life There are a variety of ways to locate a company which is compatible with your needs. Below are the strategies we have listed based on their order of their effectiveness and preferred.

Contact them: We have highlighted above in this list of text that phone calls are a miracle. Contact the manufacturer to learn about what they can provide by asking for the list of their products. Find out if they drop-ship or not. This is an essential.

Google: Google is indeed your best friend. This is evident, so why didn't we begin with this? Because, there are many aspects you should be aware of,

Conduct a thorough search: Let's go over an old argument about wholesalers not being able to market however, we will not take offense to them. That means your most popular searches may not be exactly what you're looking for. However, take this as and ask yourself, when was the most recent time you clicked 'next page' in the results of a Google search? Now you've got a reason to.

Website design and aesthetics can be deceiving The way an online site's design may be a great indicator of the seriousness of a company however, this might not pertain to suppliers, specifically wholesalers. Do not browse through a website only to move into the next since the one you were on did not appear appealing.

Make use of the most modifiers you can You've heard it enough times , so here's another chance to say it. Wholesalers don't invest in marketing and do not make any search engine optimization. You can try using many keywords that can provide the exact results you're searching for, such as warehouse, distributor wholesaler, bulk supplier, or.

Your competitors are your friends You're asking yourself: What's the deal? Your completed form can aid in finding the supplier. What do you need to ask? Simple. Make a small purchase with another company that offers drop shipping. After you receive your package, you can Google the return address in the parcel. Then, you've identified who the original recipient was of your package. Contact them again.

Expose to Trade Shows: The trade show provide an advantage in centralization. Attending trade shows allows you to meet potential suppliers all in a single location. This is only possible, however only after you've identified a market niche and have a clear idea of the product you'd like to work with.

Directorsies: We go! We advised you to not mix suppliers with directories with suppliers. What exactly is a directories? They are a list of suppliers. It's simple. They usually are sorted according to niches, markets or items. The next question is, why you should pay for directories of suppliers? The reason is that most of the businesses that operate directories for companies that are profit-oriented, so they charge you for allowing you to access their database. To avoid paying a monthly fee and other charges that are incurred by directories for suppliers, make sure that you conduct your own research and are aware of what exactly you're searching for. Find your niche market and the products you are looking for. It will take some searching to discover what you're looking for.

Here are a few directories for suppliers with excellent customer service; Doba, Wholesale Central, Worldwide Brands and SaleHoo.

Before you contact them, make sure to

After we've gone some sort of criteria to determine a potential supplier, and you're ready to reach them but there are some items that must be checked before doing this.

Are you a legal business? Are you legally registered? We've often asked that almost all wholesalers ask you to verify that your company is legally registered. They typically only disclose their pricing to registered companies that are legally registered. If you only require basic information , then you will receive it without documents, but in order to fully be incorporated into the system and gain the insider information your company must be legally valid.

Know the situation: You must be aware that your supplier won't take any additional effort and will not go one inch to assist you. Like everyone else, anyone who gets in touch with them makes promises and boasts about how fantastic their plans are. The company has heard the same thing before and they've seen everything. Every supplier needs credibility. Make sure you are clear in your claims and responses, using words like 'we've"," "we're". Make sure to mention things that carry significance and make sure to mention any experience in your profession. Be careful not to use phrases such as "I believe." Don't request favors in a hurry and make yourself as convincing as you can.

Phones are your best friend The idea of making phone calls , especially to those who are considered as superior to us is terrifying. However, phone calls are an extremely effective method to get things done. Telephone calls aren't so scary as you might think. Suppliers are also used to receiving calls, so you'll be handled.

The characteristics of a good supplier

Expert Staff: A good sign of a reputable supplier is the quality of its personnel. The best suppliers have employees who know the market well. It is evident from the way they respond to questions.

Committed support: Basically suppliers should assign you a sales rep to ensure a smooth workflow of your business. The sales representative is expected to look after, manage and meet your requirements. It can be very stressful to be forced to contact suppliers and demand they solve a particular problem. So, the sales rep acts as a mediator between the two parties.

Technology: As time passes by, the most important factor to surviving in this field is flexibility. This is a great way to identify the kind of company you're working with. If they're investing in the latest technology, they'll be great to deal with. They can provide you with live feeds of inventory as well as catalogs, shipping and other such things. Imagine a provider that does all this by hand.

Accepts orders by email: This may seem small and insignificant however, some vendors don't accept orders through email. For a second, think about the necessity of placing every single order over the phone, and whether or not that process seems to be efficient to you.

Location: In the business of drop shipping the location is among the factors that hold significant importance. Locate a provider located situated in between the nation particularly if you reside in a large country like Canada or the United States or Canada. Why? This is due to the fact that the supplier's location is in one part of the world, it could take a long time to have orders shipped to the other side of the country. The ideal fulfillment time is between two and three days, so keep this in your head.

Efficiency and organization: These is difficult to quantify and quantify. What can you tell if anyone you've never worked with is efficient and organized? Simple, you work with them. How? Make an order and then decide. This will let you know the details about drop shipping suppliers.

How to pay suppliers:

Two ways the suppliers accept payment:

Credit cards: The majority of companies will require that you make payments using a credit card when you're just starting out. If your business expands and grows but credit cards are the most suitable option for making payments as they accumulate lots of reward points.

Net Terms: net terms refers to that you get some weeks to settle the the items you have purchased. For example, if you are on "net 40' term, that means you will have forty days calculated as of the date of purchase in order to make payment for items whether by cheque or by bank.

Chapter 11: Promoting Your Shopify Store

The goal of every Shopify site is to boost the number of visitors, and the overall efficiency of conversion. If you are aware of what you want to go after, it could be difficult to determine the best marketing strategies to reach the goal. For an online store can't increase sales unless visitors to your site are very high. It's not just the amount of traffic that is important and the speed of conversion is also important. In this article we'll explore some efficient marketing strategies you can implement to advertise your Shopify store effectively online. Don't rush and don't implement all of the strategies all at once. Instead, you should take your time and implement each one at a time. This way you will be able to determine which strategies can and won't work for your company.

Before we can begin knowing how to market Shopify's Shopify store, it's essential to comprehend what is meant by e-commerce. E-commerce marketing is a straightforward technique of using a variety of ways to draw attention to a particular online store, then converting those visitors into paying customers, and keeping the customers and increasing the number of customers. A successful strategy for e-commerce consists of different marketing techniques which help to build brand awareness increase customer loyalty, and retention of customers, and ultimately, lead to an increase in overall revenue of the business. Use the strategies that are discussed in this section to market your online store, or to increase sales of a particular product.

Reduce the number of abandoned Carts

Make sure you understand that your business could be losing money every time a customer or visitor decides to leave his shopping cart without making an purchase. Many customers can add items to their carts however, they are more likely to leave the carts for a variety of reasons prior to making the purchase. Make sure to address as many of the doubts that customers might experience. The most effective way to decrease the number of carts that are abandoned is to gently remind customers about their carts that have been abandoned. Maybe you can convince customers to purchase a product with free shipping, or perhaps an offer of a discount.

An easy and effective marketing technique to decrease the amount of abandoned carts is to employ emails to recover carts. Explore the various tips that were discussed earlier in this chapter in order to build your own email lists. After your list of email addresses is set up you can contact them whenever you discover that customers on your list haven't finish a purchase or left their shopping carts off your site. For example, the message you could send to these users might be something along the lines of "Did you leave something out? You're still waiting for you in the shopping cart!" Any email response that is designed needs to be very attractive and should remind people of those juices or what prompted him to purchase the items initially.

Upselling

It is a powerful tactic which has been employed by marketers for years. It's all about raising the cart value or the amount of money you pay. You've probably seen a variation of an expression that basically says,

"Would you like to increase the value of your cart?" Instead of trying to find new customers, selling up is a great way to earn money too. In some cases customers may not be conscious of the many top products on the market or may require additional guidance on how the upgraded version is to meet their needs. For example, if you sell handmade leather products, then to increase the value of your products you can include brushes, polish for leather, or even wax, to increase the value of the cart. It is also possible to create appealing combinations that will entice buyers to boost their overall cart value. In this way, you're selling to a customer who paid $20 for one purchase, they could spend 30 dollars for the purchase. This may not seem like a lot however over time that is long, the profit through upselling will surely increase.

Two things to keep in mind when using upselling to increase profits of your business. Make sure that the product you're selling is in direct relation to or complementary to the product you are selling. The third point is to pay attention to the price range that you anticipate for the people you are targeting. The product should not just meet the needs of your client's initial requirements but also fit within the budget that the target market might not wish to go over.

Utilizing Instagram

There is no longer a time where social media was limited to Facebook. A popular and effective and popular social media platforms today is Instagram. Instagram has more than 500 million active users on a daily basis. So, why not take advantage of the huge coverage this platform provides? Making use of compelling images, using strategic hashtags, and posting when it is appropriate is a fantastic method of building the Instagram fan base for your online store. The goal is to comprehend the value that organic Instagram, and to increase your engagement with your people you follow. Therefore, it's not just about sharing photos or other content, it's also about engaging with your intended group of followers. If you can engage your audience, the higher chances they are to become paying customers.

One of the easiest methods to interact with your audience Instagram is to run contests, taking a look to the back of the house, or even demonstrating the process of product creation. Make sure you are experimenting with the various Instagram features, such as Stories, IGTV, or even the numerous challenges that continue to pop up. Make sure to keep the Instagram page fun, welcoming and fun. It should be entertaining, enjoyable and witty. Do not make your content urgent, fast, or professional. Instead, make an effort to harness the potential of social media in order to improve the exposure of your business.

The Facebook Store is launching

Facebook may not be the sole social media platform that is available in the present However, it's one you shouldn't afford to miss. The easiest way to get the most out of Facebook is by creating an online Facebook store. It's an excellent option to advertise your e-commerce store online. You can generate sales with the Facebook store. It is also possible to integrate the shop to Your Shopify store, meaning there is no need to manage the inventory separately. Making an online Facebook store is a simple procedure.

By putting an Facebook shop tab onto your page and directing users to purchase the items they like directly from your Facebook page. This is in place of opening your site. The Facebook store application is a great and inexpensive method to boost your business' visibility due to the huge customer base that Facebook gives. Facebook stores help boost sales and increase the likelihood of engaging with your customers and can help build brand recognition and brand awareness.

Wishlist Reminders

Make sure to send email reminders to the subscribers list. The reminder for your wish list is similar to an email you'd send to an abandoned cart customer. The goal of both emails is to persuade the user to buy something or encourage them to make an purchase instead of abandoning the cart completely. When a user is willing to purchase then you have to do to send a wish list email. A majority of shopping apps send out emails or notifications with the format of reminders for wish lists. Are there items available for sale that has been listed on multiple wish lists? Does the item have a high probability of selling out? Have you taken a long time since you had a look at their wish list? If you can answer yes to those questions it's the right time to send a Wish List reminder. In some cases, customers often forget about their shopping carts after a time. Remind them gently, the best method to do this is to send an email. It could be the only thing for the user to become a regular customer.

Email Campaigns

In the preceding chapter in the previous chapter, you were presented with various strategies to increase your list of email subscribers. But the addresses are going to serve your business ineffectively unless you utilize them to advertise your e-commerce store. Businesses must regularly send out valuable emails to every subscriber on their list of email addresses. There are many occasions when you can send an email as the most effective method to let your customers know gratitude to your customers and the love they have shown to your company. The easiest way to accomplish this is to send an invitation email immediately after a person purchases. Be sure to send periodic newsletters to inform all your subscribers on new products, helpful tips for using existing products, discounts, special offers and any other information suitable for your subscribers. It is also possible to use email to offer exclusive gifts or promotional coupons to all your customers. It is also possible to send relevant content to all your customers in order to ensure they make the most out of their purchases. If your content is relevant to the people you want to reach Don't be afraid to click send. But, be careful not to go overboard with your emails. Be sure to not send more than one email each week. If you are constantly bombarding your subscribers with email messages, they'll promptly unsubscribe.

Avoid poor design

If your online website isn't properly designed or poorly designed it will soon drop more sales than earn. Poorly designed websites does not just look untrustworthy however, it frequently uses complicated navigation, has an unsubstantiated proposition of value, and makes use of a sloppy font. As was mentioned in the preceding chapters, the appearance of your site is essential. It is essential when it comes to an online-based business. Because you don't have a physical storefront where your intended customers can go to the e-commerce site acts as a storefront. Make sure you take your time and don't get caught up in web design. Shopify is a easy platform to use. If you're willing to put in the time and effort required it is possible to design an attractive website using little or no technical expertise.

Be aware that regardless of how amazing the products on your site are but it's just not making sense if your customers aren't finding your site interesting or interesting. First impressions count for business online. So, make sure the overall appearance of your site is pleasing and easy to read.

Content Marketing

If you are looking to boost the visibility of your online website in search results, or you'd like to get in touch with your customers frequently you should consider blogging. If you're already pumping out content, you should consider including it in blogs that are available on your store's website. There are a variety of methods to use content marketing to your advantage, and it doesn't have to be limited to writing blogs. You can also post guest posts on other blogs or websites to increase awareness and build backlinks to your site. Start your own podcast with guests. If you'd like you could also develop long-form content that is in the form of guides or books that your intended audience will be able to use.

Utilize Content created by users

Social proofing is a must in the current world of online. The most effective way to accomplish this is to use user-generated content. When potential customers see that others, like their own, are buying products on your website frequently this increases their trust in your company. One method that is the most efficient to utilize user-generated content is to ask customers to share photos of in which they're using the items you offer. For example, if you sell footwear or clothing you could invite your customers to share photos on their social media profiles wearing your items and tag your company. This isn't as simple as reviews and testimonials can help increase your social proof, however, this tactic is effective.

Personalization Matters

If you want to boost the sales on your website personalization is an efficient method. Utilizing the data from your customers' behavior that you collect, you can provide customized experiences to all of your visitors. There aren't many businesses that know about this technique. Try to get the most benefit from it now. It is also possible to use location to customize or create an experience specifically catering to the needs of customers. It is located in a particular region around the world. For instance, if you're website is selling bathing suits, make sure you offer discounts and specials prior to when the spring season begins. There is also the possibility that someone within Southern California might be looking for bathing suits in the month of October, whereas those in Maine might be searching for winter clothes.

Reward Customers Who Stay Loyal

It's not enough to acquire more customers but to be able to keep in touch with your loyal ones. Your most loyal customers are brand advocates that they are free. If you're doing an excellent job with your customers and you have an established client base do not forget to show your appreciation to them. Let them know that you are grateful for their ongoing assistance and friendship. There are many ways to give a gift to loyal customers or customers who spend a lot by establishing loyalty programs for customers. You can offer them additional incentives each time they purchase something or provide them with the first priority when you have offers being offered through your website. Everyone wants to feel unique and special. If you offer your loyal customers a special services, the odds that they will remain loyal will grow.

Be aware that you're the only person who can determine what, when and for how much you want to reward your customers. You could develop a point-based program for your store in which certain points will be added to a customer's account every time they make purchases. After accumulating a set amount in points customer is able to redeem them for every subsequent purchase. Also, you can offer special offers for a limited time such as free shipping or other basic freebies to show appreciation to customers who have been loyal to you for your loyalty to your business.

If you follow the easy tips that are provided in this chapter, you can increase your web's visibility, traffic, and even the sales your company achieves. However, bear your mind in the forefront that it requires constant effort and time to achieve the desired results from these tactics. Be patient, be attentive to the outcomes, and constantly alter the strategies to meet the demands of your company.

Chapter 12: The Tax Rates And Shipping

If you're selling physical goods it's not over until the item has been delivered to the buyer and the customer is satisfied. The time spent to properly set up your shipping process and get yourself ready to ship the item can help reduce the time spent on the process. The ideal scenario is that you provide many options for shipping possible for the customer to pick from. So they will receive their goods at the most affordable prices or at the most appropriate dates.

Manual Shipping Costs

Manual shipping rates are fixed prices applied to each item. When you set a manual rate customers will be able to be aware of the price of shipping and you are able to send the item out in any way you wish when it is delivered to the buyer. It is recommended to include the estimated delivery times to assist customers.

The benefit of this method is that you don't need to weigh each itemindividually, however, the drawbacks are numerous. The customers are not able of deciding the way in which an item is delivered (what do they do if they want faster delivery?) However, they could be shocked in the event that your shipping costs are more expensive than it has to be. If your customers buy several items the fixed rate might not be able to accommodate the dimensions of the box needed to deliver them all at one time. In general, this isn't the best option to choose.

The main drawback is that you could underestimate your costs incorrectly. If the shipping costs exceed the fixed price that you've established, you'll need to pay for the additional by yourself. This is fine if include the cost of shipping and other materials into the price of your product However, you should be cautious regarding how you price your products.

If you're only selling one product line, and they're all the same weight and size it could be a viable option. If not it, you should provide shipping options to customers.

Shopify USPS Shipping

Similar to eBay as well as PayPal, Shopify has a agreement with the USPS that lets you purchase labels at a discount price and print them at home. Since you're most likely to sell products that range from small to huge from light to heavy and heavy, this will likely to be the most efficient option. The only thing you have to do is to set up a weight perhaps a little larger than the actual weight , to be able to accommodate the packaging materials and handling.

If the customer is able to pay the payment, they have the option of choosing one of the USPS choices that allow customers to pay more to receive faster service. Shopify will automatically take the weight and size of your parcel into account and won't allow the customer to purchase first-class mail in cases where it's not appropriate therefore there's no need to worry about not being compensated enough for shipping charges If your weights are in order. Also, the reduced prices (based on the tier you're using of Shopify you choose to use) will help you save money. If you're a seller with a lot of volume which is what we all hope to be and the Professional Plan's lower costs will help you save a substantial portion of your money over a time.

Other Carriers

You could also offer alternative shipping providers to your customers, such as UPS and FedEx as well as other. If you use the shipping settings in the settings it is possible to integrate shipping APIs that allow the calculation of these costs to be done much similar to how USPS cost is calculated. There's no discount in Shopify and these companies however, if you have an account for business with UPS like, for instance the discount will be applicable. However, it's only available to Professional member, which , if you recall is $299.99 per month. For sellers who are high volume it's worthwhile to have these extra options.

Fulfilment and Dropshipping

Dropshipping has been mentioned briefly We'll go over more in depth later. It could be the most efficient option for shipping since the goods aren't even being purchased by you until they're being sold directly to the buyer!

Fulfillment shipping is another option it is similar in the sense that you're not taking care of the shipping, however unlike dropshipping you've bought the item and are now keeping them with an organisation that will deliver them to you when they are sold. This option could yield better results than regular dropshipping but you're still investing into the product and in the fulfilment company's time. The best option is to locate a local fulfilment service that can get your the products delivered without much hassle.

Shipping Settings

After we've discussed the shipping options and payment options, it's time to proceed with creating it. We went through this process briefly in the "Settings" section of the Shopify interface and you might have this in mind in the event that you've taken time to investigate.

Go into the "Settings" page, then select "Shipping."

You'll find various things you can alter. This includes:

Shipping Origin The shipping origin is the address for return. Most likely, it is your home address , unless you have a designated business address. If you do not wish to have your home address to appear on the label, you can open a PO Box at the local post office in order to avoid this. Don't use a fake address.

Tariffs and zones - Here you are able to set up your shipping zones and rates. This also includes the option to restrict shipping to specific regions of the world. In default, everything is included, therefore it is advisable to change this if you don't intend to provide international shipping. Within the manual rates for shipping.

Label format - Then you'll be able to see the format of labels. If you're using specific printing equipment or labeling, you'll be able to alter this according to your requirements. When you're working with a laser printer or an inkjet printer, which is standard and you're just taping labels, you can keep it as it is.

Packaging - If there is several boxes that you can use to transport your items by inserting the sizes of these boxes can help reduce the time required to enter the information needed for future products.

Additional Shipping Methods It is here that you set up methods that are not the calculated USPS rates.

Shipping the Product

Once an order has been placed, Shopify will notify you (unless you have disabled notification) After the order is placed, they'll offer you the option of printing the shipping label. If you're using standard calculated shipping method, the label will automatically correspond to the information you've provided to calculate shipping. You can alter the label as necessary. Make sure the measurements and weights are in order.

In order to ship your items, you'll require the following items:

Bubble mailers or boxes in different sizes that work to the products you have. If you're only selling just a handful of items available for sale You can put off on purchasing in large quantities, but when you start moving items, it is essential to have the standard packaging materials in stock to make the process easier.

Padding, like bubble wrap and newspapers. Peanuts for packing are becoming less frequent and is recommended to avoid them because the majority of customers consider them to be insensitive for the environment.

Shipping tape. Ideally, it should be transparent. So, if you're printing labels onto paper and then gluing them onto boxes, it is possible that you are able to tape them over a little but without obscuring the message. Be aware that you are not allowed to cover the barcodes. It's not a problem in the event that you do, but it's technically forbidden from the USPS.

Printer for printing labels.

Paper or label paper. Label paper is adhesive-backed so you just peel it off and stick it on the box after it's printed. After a product has been labeled, you can bring it into the Post Office, or you can sign in at USPS and request a pickup.

If you're using third-party service providers make sure to check with them to make sure you're following their guidelines. They will usually provide home pickup, too. If you're using fulfillment services, Shopify and the service can assist you in setting this up in a manner which will make it easier to process the shipments afterward.

Shipping Costs and Order Fulfillment

To set your shipping costs From the control panel of your account, click "Shipping." You can input the rates and locations you'd like, but it is easiest to set two rates - a home country rate and an "Rest of the world" rate.

On the next page, you will find options to add Drop shipping or order fulfillment. They aren't

Shopify's services are managed by third-party companies - many of which are well-known names. It is a wonderful method to sell your goods across the globe without having to ship packages yourself. Drop shipping company loads of your merchandise and they handle everything to you - storage for stock packaging, posting and storage. Additionally, since Shopify is able to integrate seamlessly into these platforms, you'll be able to ensure that your orders can be handled by another firm without your involvement in the process.

Tax Rates

If your earnings exceed the threshold of a certain amount in many countries where VAT or tax mechanisms in effect. If taxes must be added to your orders, simply click "Tax" within the admin main panel, and put in the appropriate tax amount into the box marked "Country tax rate." The tax will be added to invoices and you'll be able to view the tax you paid in those sales records. If you don't need to collect tax it is possible to be set to zero.

To access tax returns To view tax reports, click on "Reports" after which click click on "Tax Ratio."

Chapter 13: The Mistakes To Avoid

Are you just beginning to get started in the world of e-commerce? It can be a bit overwhelming. procedure can seem intimidating, and starting your first business may seem like a daunting undertaking. But, with time you will find it more manageable. Making mistakes is an essential part of the process. You don't have to fail to be able to learn. You can gain a lot from the mistakes made by others as well. Let's examine one of the frequently made Shopify mistakes and tips to avoid these.

Utilizing the default Settings

Focusing on SEO is a must in order to boost popularity of your web shop or products that you offer. To improve your SEO rating be sure to avoid the default options to use Meta tags. Therefore, each blog post, page and product should be manually inserted into the Meta tags to improve the SEO of your website. When you make changes to an item or a webpage then, you can click on your Edit Website SEO option at the end of your page, and click on Edit Meta Information. If you do

125

not complete this step, all the 160 character characters of your collection, webpage or product's page will be assigned to be the title that is default. SEO isn't only important for increasing your online visibility however, it also gives you the user with a better experience.

Inadequacy in a Uniform Theme

The different colors that are available on the Shopify theme should match the colors of the color scheme of your store's colors. Always double-check for uniformity of the colors. For instance, any links that you click to your website should be the same color. Take a careful look at the different settings and configurations of your website to ensure that all essential information is displayed in a consistent manner. To ensure an experience that is consistent for your customers take the time to review the options of your online store.

There is no brand

The credibility of your business on the market is reflected by its logo. Even if your online site is launched at a broad range, it's possible that your brand will not have a large fan base if it does not have an identity. What's the first thing that comes to your brain when you see the bright yellow M? It could be a thought of McDonald's. Therefore, don't undervalue brand recognition and always include a logo that can create instant recognition for your business. If you aren't sure you're equipped to design the logo do not hesitate to seek professionals.

Improper Contact Information

The about us page or the contact page is an essential element for any online store or site. It's a page you shouldn't overlook in order to become an effective e-commerce store owner. It is the About Us page is your company's first introduction to prospective customers. The page outlines the mission, vision and the value proposition of your business as well as the unique selling feature. Include details about contact information such as telephone number, email address actress, fax numbers and a PO box address if appropriate.

Checkout Page It's important

There are numerous choices for customizing checkout page templates on Shopify. So, make sure to be sure to check the checkout pages of the site prior to launching the store. When you view the site or the online store from the perspective of a consumer and you'll gain more insight into factors that work and those that don't help you. It is essential for a checkout system that for your online store is quick and painless. The design of your checkout site should be similar to other pages on your e-commerce store. Additionally, make sure the font is consistent across the site. The checkout page shouldn't look like an unintentional extension of your online store Shopify store.

The Font Selection should be limited. Selection

Shopify has a range of fonts. Choosing the perfect font for your online store could be a bit intimidating. When choosing one, you should make sure to choose at minimum two or three fonts. Then, you can choose one that is compatible with the brand name and your store's name. It is possible to create a range of designs using a single font because of the many options available including bold letters, spacing between letters thin, italics and standard styles. If you are looking to give a professional and clear appearance to your online store The font style should be consistent across your website. You can't apply one font style to the page, only to change it for other pages. If you also use several fonts on one page, it can make the site look chaotic.

Do not overlook the Soft Launch

Prior to lining up for an official opening, you can opt for an unofficial launch of the online store. With a soft launch, present your site or online store to a small amount of people. Before the site is made available to everyone, you should make an unintentional launch. If you conduct this, you'll get an overview of the various features of your site that function but don't help its users. Utilize the feedback you get from a soft launch and you'll be able to make necessary changes prior to when the site is launched. Soft launches are similar to the screening of a selected film before the actual release.

We do not offer multiple payment options

If you wish to increase the sales value and the amount of customers your shop attracts it is essential to provide a range different payment methods. Don't limit your options to just one payment processor and offer some choices. If you are able to offer just two or three payment options, don't assume that every potential customer has to utilize those same gateways.

Insufficient Marketing Plan

You won't be able to reap the full benefit of the benefits provided by Shopify without a solid marketing strategy in place. It provides guidelines for your ideal customer and selling strategies, business coach, and even the setup for your promotional campaign. A solid marketing plan will provide comprehensive information about not only your ideal target customer, but the entire selling cycle as well. One way to put together a marketing plan is to identify your brand's identity and USP as well as your intended market, the various tactics you use to promote your brand and the objectives you're planning to pursue.

Inefficiency

Landing pages can be different from the normal pages that you can find on your website. A landing page has specific purposes. Its purpose is determined by the source that directs your intended audience to the site. Most often the Landing Page helps generate leads and help increase the number of calls to action, while also providing details about the product or service, or item sold. Your landing pages must be optimized to the max, lead the customer to the correct direction, and should execute a specific task. A great landing page must help visitors, you to the right mail addresses, cross sell or even upselland draw some interest in the products or services your business has to offer.

Beware of First-Time Visitors

Don't think about the power of a great first impression. First impressions count a lot especially when it involves selling and selling on the internet, particularly. The one mistake you need to stay clear of at all cost is not making the best impression to a new customer to your online store. The first impression that your store makes on them will determine if they'll stay on and close a deal or leave the site. There are a few things that you should consider when creating the most memorable first impression include the message that your website's landing page conveys and the color scheme you use and pop-ups that you make use of and the methods you employ to engage visitors. If your website looks attractive and makes your visitors feel appreciated, or provides important information and offers your chances of conversion are higher.

A lack of awareness

You won't be successful as a business owner if you're not sure of your audience. When you are considering launching your venture, take the time to think about who is my intended market? Whatever your concept is but you will not be able to successfully market your idea if you don't have people willing to buy it. So, you need to be aware of the ideal customers. A perfect customer is someone who is most likely purchase any product or service your website provides. If you are able to establish a clear understanding regarding your intended audience and preferences, you can select the most appropriate products and focus on a personalised and individualized marketing strategy.

Avoid PPC Ads

Paid per Click or PPC advertisements are an amazing method of generating leads and boost conversions. However, many often overlook or undervalue the power PPC ads provide. It's not that difficult to put in the work or energy to create an effective PPC campaign. If you're in it for the long haul and want to be successful, you must not overlook the significance of PPC advertising campaigns. A PPC campaign can bring in leads and traffic more rapidly than SEO organic traffic. It also lets you evaluate and alter the budget of your ads according to the return on investment. If you're PPC campaign is properly planned you can cut down on your cost per visit. Additionally, you can utilize the PPC advertisement to test A/B and shut down a campaign if you aren't getting the desired outcomes.

It is essential to have a lot of experience and understanding before you can start the most successful PPC advertising campaign. If you're new with Shopify There are a few applications that you can utilize to incorporate PPC ads into your online store. The most widely used options include Google advertising as well as Google shopping. It is also possible to utilize adNabu as well as other third-party software to design and connect an PPC advertisement into your online store Shopify story.

Inattention to Accounting

The importance of accounting should not be undervalued. Be aware that you're launching an enterprise, like any other enterprise tracking your financial accounts is crucial. Invoicing, bookkeeping, taxes and tracking expenses all matter. If you don't keep an accurate account of this in your accounting, you may find yourself overestimating or underestimating the amount of money you earn. In addition, to remain on top of all taxes due, it is essential to have a sound accounting system in place. If you do not want to run into legal issues Don't overlook the importance of accounting in depth. There are a variety of applications online, as well as accounting automation software and software that you can employ to track all your accounts. If you're looking for a more traditional approach to go with the traditional route and record the journals of your accounts. If you're not sure if you have the ability to handle accounting, you could hire an expert to assist you in all this.

Chapter 14: What To Take Into Consideration Before Getting Started

Before you begin building your own website for e-commerce there are certain aspects you should consider. Consider asking yourself if you're capable of handling the following duties that are required when managing this type of company.

Are you prepared to commit the time required to manage a successful online business? Although you'll eventually be the sole proprietor of your business and be in control of setting your own hours of work but you'll still be faced with the obligation of working a few additional hours each week to set your site, probably over and above your other work in the meantime. Even after your website is in place you'll need to set aside time for storage information on updates, shipping obligations and communication between your company and customers, and keeping track of developments in the industry that relate to your product.

* Can you afford for investment in the store while as well as juggling other financial

obligations? Additionally, are you prepared to compromise downtime to meet the financial obligations necessary for the establishment of your business? Be conscious of the financial risk of this kind of goal and ensure you're financially ready, or have a plan of recovery in case something doesn't succeed.

* Are you able to put money into your business for a period of a year or more without making a significant profits? As per the Small Business Administration, most small businesses don't begin making significant profits after the third or second year of operation. Be sure that you're financially and willing to invest this length of time to a business before you receive the benefits of your investment.

Do you think of staying committed to your business even if you don't get immediate outcomes? One of the major reason why only a small percentage of those who want to establish their own company actually achieve success is that they quit once they hit a bump on the road. Are you able to continue moving forward, despite other obligations and the possibility of short-term setbacks to your company?

* Are you prepared to be willing to fail with your company? In spite of your best efforts and determination to make your business a success there's a probable possibility that it won't be successful eventually and you'll have to make the choice of cutting losses. This happens. You will encounter fierce competitors and it requires an enormous amount of luck to manage an online store that is successful. If your venture is successful, it is bound to be lucrative and lucrative, however, make sure you're prepared to risk the fact that you will never get to that point.

Why starting an online store is a good idea

While the above precautions might make the idea of launching your own e-commerce site seem like an undesirable option for a career, there's still plenty of benefit in making this a life-altering decision. It's true that getting to the point at which your company is a steady and profitable achievement isn't easy, with enough risks that it could appear as if that it's not worth it However, there are plenty of beneficial benefits that make taking on the risk worth it.

You'll be the boss of your life. As the creator of a highly successful online shop, you can be as busy and as few hours as you'd like. With the endless profits that will be made yours and your employees, you can employ an entire team of people to run the website on your behalf, should you wish while making an amazing profits. As the founder, you'll are in complete control of your business's operations as well as the liberty to do whatever you wish with this control.

* You can run your business from the comfort of your home. One of the greatest benefits of running a business that is online is the ability to work at home. There's no need for alarms in the morning suits, traffic, or even suits. Instead, you can enjoy the option of getting out of the bed (or even sleeping in!) and accessing your website while wearing your PJs. This freedom lets you to work from home whenever you'd like, without need to call in or make a plan essential. If you're not the only person who manages the transactions with clients There is nothing that can stop you

from adjusting your schedule to meet your preferences and requirements.

* Your earnings will be unlimited. There is a chance to earn a significant amount of money with your site. A website that sells products online offers the chance to make money that paying a few checks (with an occasional raise in the event of luck) will not be enough. It's very likely that your site could transform you into millionaire. If your business is successful you'll want nothing.

* You'll have a head start on the pack. Ecommerce is the direction that the future is heading in terms of a successful business. Shopping online is becoming increasingly frequent each year, and conventional retail shops are getting less frequent. In a time that online shopping could soon become one of the biggest, and if certainly not profitable businesses, you'll want to make sure you get onto the wave and get on the receiving profit as soon as you can to benefit from this upcoming change in culture.

The benefits of creating your Shopify Store Yourself Shopify Store

There are distinct advantages when you create an e-commerce site by using Shopify instead of. simply making your own online store. In particular the Shopify platform helps reduce the risk you'll face when developing your website. If you're ready to start your own e-commerce site Shopify is the best option to succeed. Here's why.

* Cost. It typically costs many thousands to create the type of website you'd require to be successful in this type of business. When you pay a web designer who has the right skills and a programmer who is able to program the functions of your site and set up security features, you'll be billed a substantial quantity of dollars before you begin to create any. Shopify provides an option where you pay a certain and clearly-described cost, and choose between four different levels to create the ideal e-commerce site for your needs.

* Support. When you create an e-commerce site using Shopify it comes with the assistance of the Shopify staff. Utilizing the Shopify platform will let you skip all the bugs and faults that can arise when you create the website from scratch They will not cause any

problems in your website, and you won't require a lot of time and money to fix the issues. Shopify has been through the initial stages of design for websites, and it now has bug-free options to allow you to take a branch from for your own company. Additionally, the platform provides elements to allow you to create your platform as soon after registering your account. Help pages are provided to help you set up more complex settings, however, the creation of a website is quite simple.

* Security. Shopify has security built-in, but it does not guarantee security when you build your website from scratch. In addition, Shopify's security features are top-rated with a score that is higher than other e-commerce platforms on the market. Shopify lets you can avail some of the top security features without having to pay for it out of your pocket.

* Traffic. Web page designers who build websites from scratch usually invest a lot of money in features to increase traffic. When you create your website using Shopify your company has the chance to be among the first results that appear on search engines.

Naturally the most popular results are the ones that bring in the most traffic.

* Marketing. Shopify's tools are also helpful in marketing your product by focusing on the interests of your customers and tracking their activities to determine the most effective way to encourage customers to remain on your website once they have arrived. All you need to do is make sure you have the best merchandise to offer when Shopify determines what it is that they want to purchase from you. Up until then Shopify handles all marketing elements and draws in the customers that's the first step to having an effective online store that Shopify takes by Shopify.

* Mobile optimization. The Shopify platform is already optimized to be mobile-friendly by your customers, which means you'll have a site that is accessible on every device. This is especially important as smartphones and tablets are rapidly becoming the most popular gadgets used to shop. Shopify's mobile optimization is set to be upgraded as new technological advancements take place which means you don't have the worry of

losing contact with potential customers in the field.

* Hosting. Since your website for e-commerce is hosted by Shopify it is not necessary to think about adding features to your purchases and transactions. This is beneficial since you won't need to set the technical issues by yourself. In addition, you'll are able to save money that you needed to invest in security, as well as the bandwidth required to handle the traffic of your customers, which is already handled by your hosting provider, Shopify.

* Reliability. Shopify certainly is able to live up to its reputation as the most reputable e-commerce platform available. The reason for its popularity is due to its trustworthiness for its customers. If you build your own website starting from scratch, you could end up spending time identifying and fixing issues that could instead be used to increase more traffic and earning money. Shopify has gone through this initial trial and error phase and now offers a secure platform to help you achieve success with your business. It's not necessary to worry about closing your

website to fix issues instead of making money.

Accessibility to apps. Shopify offers a variety of apps that can help you run your store. Shopify's app store provides applications that provide you with statistics, send reminders for shipping and provide customized printing, to mention just a few.

Chapter 15: Set Up Shopify

Filling your Estore with the latest merchandise

If your product is physical item (digital and subscription-based products do not require keeping the inventory) and it's not something you can make by yourself -- like art knitting blankets and knitted clothing or jewelry, you have to locate a way to fill your store with the desired product. It involves two difficult actions: finding a reliable supplier , and one that is willing to offer the product at a price that is low enough in order to earn enough money without overpricing yourself. This is known as buying the product wholesale.

Wholesale Purchases of Wholesale Products

Unfortunately, purchasing the items you want for your store to stock it with isn't as simple as we'd wish it to be. It is not a simple process of going from the manufacturer to the owner of the store. Instead, it is passed through the manufacture to the distributor. The distributor then transfers it to the wholesaler. The wholesaler, then (although sometimes there are additional steps) then sells the product to the retailer you! At this point, the price of the item is typically increased considerably from the time of purchase since just like you, every other buyer has to earn a profit. Additionally, many wholesalers won't sell to you if you do not purchase a certain amount of the product, or they may not offer it to you at all unless they are a larger business. Due to this, you'll have to commit an enormous amount of time creating and maintaining relations with suppliers to reap the maximum benefit and minimize stress when you stock up your shop.

Where do the wholesale products originate

Wholesale companies control over about 1/4 of the industry, making it in fact a requirement to be a part of it in order to operate an online store. In the upper tier of the chain, the producers produce the products that is then shipped into the U.S. The distributors then sell their products to retailers in certain regions, or , sometimes, to brokers who purchase the products for retailers.

Finding the Most Value Deal

To get the most affordable price when buying your goods, you need to take two steps purchase in bulk and develop relationships to your supplier. A good relationship with a wholesaler could provide a low cost on products that otherwise would be prohibitively expensive to purchase in the near future, which implies you will have having more money in your savings account. A relationship like this won't be established in a hurry, of course however it is ideal to begin with a solid foundation at the start. Wholesalers appreciate it when retailers purchase wholesale, so do this frequently and you'll soon be chatting with wholesalers from the business and that's nothing less than a benefit to both you and your business.

How to locate Wholesalers

The best way to find wholesalers, and probably the most efficient method, is to search for them on the internet. Similar to the way you promote yourself to your clients wholesalers also spend lots of time, effort and money advertising to you and the retailer, which means that you'll be successful in finding them by typing their industry in the search box. Additionally there are directories devoted to the search for wholesalers like Wholesale Central.

TIP: Reach out to other stores selling the same products. Ask for recommendations. Naturally, any shop that sells a product that is too similar may not be willing to assist you since you are their competitor, so be cautious and look for stores that aren't directly competing with you.

Another approach you could consider to find wholesalers attending trade shows, which are usually attended by wholesalers. If you are unable to attend the actual show it is possible to read trade publications to determine whether you are able to find any advertisements from wholesalers that might be selling your product. There are also companies that you can visit and request recommendations, such as those at the Small Business Development Center and the regional chamber of commerce. Manufacturers themselves may offer some helpful suggestions regarding wholesalers.

Picking the right Shopify package to Meet Your Needs

In the introduction of this article, Shopify provides you with various packages you can select from. Each package is tailored to the specific requirements that an owner of an online store would require, based on the budget, the kind of store you're searching for, as well as the tools and features you require to build the kind of store you'd like to have. Here is a comprehensive overview on the Shopify features available through the platform and the related packages. From there, you'll be able to decide the features you want to be able to use for your store and what package is best for your needs.

At the time of this book's publication at the time of publication, Shopify's packages are priced as follows: Shopify packages come with the following prices:

* Lite: $9 per month

* Basic: $29 per month

* Pro: $79 per month

* Unlimited: $179 per month

These characteristics, costs and limitations:

It is only the Basic, Pro and Unlimited packages include the Shopify online store; the Lite package doesn't.

* The Point-of-Sale option that lets you accept payments with any method you choose, is included in all four plans.

*The Facebook Integration feature is also offered with the four plans. It lets visitors visit your website, they will see all the items you have in your store that is updated in real-time and given with a direct link to your online store in case they decide to purchase something.

* Pinterest Integration, similar to Shopify Integration, like the Shopify store, comes in only the Basic Pro, Premium as well as Unlimited packages, and not that Lite package. You can sell your items on Pinterest by adding a purchase button to your pinterest pins.

* Twitter Integration is another feature accessible for all packages, however Lite and serves a similar purpose as the Pinterest as well as Facebook Integration, but for twitter.

This Buy Button is available in each package. It allows you to include a Buy Button on any site.

*The Retail Package add-on is available for each plan, however it is priced at $0 per utilize.

* The rates charged by credit cards for purchases made with credit cards are different for the package. In the Lite and Basic packages it costs 2.9 percent with 30 cents on the internet, and 2.7 percent plus zero cents at the counter. The Pro package is 2.6 percent and 30 cents for online, and 2.4 percent plus zero cents at the counter. The Unlimited package costs 2.4 percent with 30 cents on the internet, and 2.2 percent plus zero cents at the counter.

* Transaction Fees are applicable to all packages, however they are not applicable unless you utilize other payment gateways for which you'll be charged 2% when you

purchase packages like the Lite or Basic packages and 1% for the Pro package, and only .5 percent for Unlimited. Unlimited package.

* The number of products allowed is indefinite for each package. Basic, Lite Pro Unlimited

24 hour support included in every package.

shipping label discounts are available for every package however, the discounts are higher with the tier of package. Lite and Basic offer the possibility of 50% off and Pro offers 55% off, and Unlimited, up to 60 percent off.

Tools for Fraud Analysis are included for each package, and will guarantee that you won't be the buyer of fraudulent products by your customers.

* Manual Order Creation feature is another option included with every package . It permits the user to create an order without requiring the customer to buy it.

The features for Blogging and Website are included in Basic Pro, Professional and

Unlimited and permit you to blog on Shopify. Shopify platform. This, as we've mentioned earlier will help you establish authority and establish yourself as an expert in the field you are interested in as well as gaining keywords to use in Google search results.

* The storage for files is provided in every package and is unlimitable.

Discount Coupons are included in each package and provide discounts to your customers if they can access the discount code. This feature can be useful in monitoring the sources of traffic to your site and helping you determine which ads had the greatest successful.

Gift Cards are available for all packages but also Lite. You can provide your customers with gift cards for your store that they can utilize themselves or to give to others and spread awareness about the store!

*The Professional Reports feature is only available in only the Pro or Unlimited packages. It lets you create advanced reports for your store, whereas the Basic package gives you a restricted report.

This feature is available only with Unlimited and has more than the earlier feature.

*The Abandoned Cart Recovery feature is available only to Pro and Unlimited and lets customers go back to their shopping carts after closing the browser.

*The Real Time Carrier Shipping feature is only available to unlimited packages.

Comparing Shopify with other platforms for e-commerce

If you're looking through this guide, it's evident that you are thinking of Shopify as the platform to host your online shop. This book is not only designed to instruct you about running an efficient e-commerce store however, it is intended to help you understand the advantages that come with Shopify over other platforms for ecommerce. To provide you with an honest and balanced review, we'll go over some of the most popular platforms and will also discuss every one of their benefits and disadvantages in comparison to Shopify.

What exactly does the definition of an Ecommerce Platform?

Ecommerce platforms are software application that gives you an example of how to build an online shop. It eliminates the majority of difficult tasks involved in making a new website including writing code and managing the intricate aspects of designing the website. Your job is to personalize the site to suit your needs by picking from a wide range of pre-designed designs that are free of bugs.

Stacking Shopify with Other Ecommerce Platforms

Shopify is without doubt the most used e-commerce platform available in the midst of hundreds, if not thousands, of other platforms. But this doesn't necessarily suggest that it's the best. In this article, we'll compare Shopify against the other three platforms which include Magento, BigCommerce and Volusion -each of which is joined by Shopify as one of the top five platforms available in the market. We'll concentrate on eight major characteristics: pricing and design customization security, features marketing, reports extensions and support, and at the end, you'll hopefully have a clear and impartial opinion about which platform is best.

* Pricing. In terms of cost, Magento is the cheapest since it's completely free, except if you opt to purchase an Enterprise Edition, which is rather expensive. BigCommerce costs the most of the three, since it has four levels of packages similar to what Shopify does, however, the cost per month for each is approximately twice that of Shopify's. The prices for Volusion are identical to Shopify's.

• Design customization. Each platform has customized designs can be made available through many themes. Some of these themes are completely free, while others cost the price of. BigCommerce does not charge any fees for its themes, however the quality of these themes isn't great. Volusion also, as usual is similar to Shopify in cost of themes and quality. It has a handful of themes at no cost and an extensive selection of premium themes that are of similar quality to Shopify's. Magento offers a variety of themes for free, but the high-quality themes cost money and are costly. Shopify and Volusion maintain the most optimal balance between cost and quality.

Frontend Features. All of these platforms are quite similar with regards to features available on the frontend. One platform in the group that may be short is BigCommerce due to its lack of organization. But, it makes its way up by providing greater features than the three other platforms, including Shopify.

* Backend Features. Contrary to the frontend it's not lacking in BigCommerce in terms of the backend. The platform provides a variety of options for customization, and an easy-to-use interface that lets you create a store that looks and feel just like your personal. Shopify is the second option, with an intuitive interface. Volusion and Magento have backends that can be more difficult to wrap your brain around and will take some time to become familiar with.

* Security. This is the area in which Shopify takes the lead to become the top platform.

The hosting offered by Shopify is top-quality and comes with an integrated content Delivery Network (CDN) and is PCI certified. BigCommerce is second and is secure, however it doesn't have the CDN. Volusion offers hosting as well as an CDN and PCI conformity, however you will need purchase the encryption Shopify provides at no cost. If you use Magento, you'll need to buy hosting outside of the platform which means you'll have to pay out of pocket, however since the base version of the platform isn't a cost anything , it evens it out.

* Marketing. Marketing doesn't just refer to advertising, but also includes SEO, social media and many other aspects. As always, BigCommerce delivers the best quality since the platform's amazing capabilities for customization extends to SEO-specific customization. Magento is second-best offering everything you need to use SEO already built in and ready to go. Shopify is the only one that offers basic SEO tools and Volusion has much less. Both platforms appear to be equal in terms of integration with social media is concerned, except for Magento and BigCommerce, which don't have

the feature. Volusion and Magento have a newsletter service, and Shopify and BigCommerce provide the option to integrate with third-party companies.

* Promotions. Each platform provides about the identical types of promotions. They all also offer tools to help you increase the amount of visitors.

* Reports. Each platform is basically in the same league in this area.

* Add-ons. Each of the four platforms has extensions that offer you the possibility of using more features than you initially were able to use. Each platform comes with an app store that you can browse through and download from. It's difficult to choose the most suitable platform in this particular category since applications are constantly changing, and it is difficult to compare the different platforms against one another in the event that they never remain the same.

* Support. With Shopify you're guaranteed all-hours support regardless of the package. BigCommerce provides 24 hour assistance on weekdays, and selected times on weekends,

and also an education center for builders of e-commerce. Volusion provides support through live chat, telephone and email at all times, whereas Magento isn't able to provide proper support unless you purchase the costly package upgrade. If you don't it is possible to visit the forum on the website for assistance and assistance.

The Initial Setup

We've discussed in detail about the things you should do in preparation to set up your online shop, however we've not yet talked about the best practices for starting the Shopify store's setting up. This chapter will guide your through all the stages for the initial set-up using Shopify beginning with joining the platform.

Disclaimer: Although as of publication, the information provided is accurate and up-to-date, Shopify may update its platform in the future and diverge from these rules. The good news is that it's a good thing that the Shopify platform is easy to use, and you shouldn't be having any problems, even after an upgrade to your system.

Signing up

You can sign up for Shopify at the following address: http://www.shopify.com. You'll be offered the option of having access for free to the platform for a trial period of two weeks. This lets you be certain that Shopify is the best choice for your needs as a business without having to invest any money upfront. In order to try the trial for free it's only necessary to supply three bits of information including your name, email address, and the title of the shop. The name of your business could be a placeholder in case you're not able to decide on a name that is permanent now, because you have the option of going back and alter the name later.

The Shopify Interface

Shopify's Shopify interface is easy and simple to use. It's layout is similar as Wordpress that is used by the majority of people. There are numerous sections on the left sidebar each of them serving different purposes.

* Search. The most prominent function of the sidebar, it lets you find everything you require to locate on your site, be it that is as broad as

a product you offer or more specific than a specific customer.

* Home. This function allows you to have the ability to access the home page.

* Orders. This section is comprised of three separate sections. This is where you can view the completed, incomplete or abandoned orders received from customers. Also, you can access the Drafts section, which allows you to mail your own invoices, orders and other documents.

* Products. Here you can can add the product descriptions in your online store. You can control your inventory, keep track of inbound products, and look over your inventory reports. The section on Products will be further discussed in the future.

* Customers. This section will help to keep on top of your customers' purchases and provides a wealth of details about their names, such as their name as well as their previous purchases at your store, location and, if they are provided photos of them looking.

* Reports. You are able to run reports on virtually every aspect of your business to ensure that you are operating at the highest efficiency. You'll be able determine where your marketing is getting attention and which areas are not and which products are most well-known and those that are not so popular. Here are a few of the reports that you can check on your store's performance:

* Your customers have been referred by referrals

* The devices used to connect to your store

* The locations of your customers

* Analyzing your customers' carts and shopping habits

* Tax reports

* Payment methods

* Sales reports

* Discounts. This is where you are able to create promotional codes and reward program for the customers you serve. Shopify

gives you three different options to offer discount coupons to your clients.

1. Percentage discounts. Your customers will receive an amount of discount off the purchase. You are able to decide what that percentage will be , and the discounts that are offered. You can also choose who gets the discount.

2. Dollar amount discount. Instead of a percentage discount it is instead an amount off of the product. Similar to the earlier type of discount, you are in the option of deciding how much will be discounted, what items it is discounted, and for whom the discount is offered to.

3. Free shipping discount. In lieu of going to the item the discount will save the buyer money on cost of shipping for the product. It is possible to select offering this discount to U.S. orders or for international orders and when discount is applicable.

• Online Store. This is the area that you can make changes to and also where you create your store.

* Apps. This section will help you manage the applications you utilize for your website. Many are free, however, certain cost between a few dollars, ranging from the 20 dollar range, and even more.

* Settings. The final section allows you to manage the smallest details regarding your store, from its name to the shipping options and payment options.

Add Products to Your Store

In a previous article, we talked about where to find your products. It is now time to consider how you can include your items to your online store. It is one of the most tedious elements of setting up the store, particularly if you have to add each product manually. Below are some tips for how you can start adding your products into your shop as efficiently swiftly and easily as is possible.

"Products Section "Products" Section

There are two sub-sections of the section on products, that are as follows:

This tutorial. It is located under the 'Learn more about Products options in the product section. You will then be directed to the video tutorial. You will discover that there are 19 components. However, you will be taught everything you need to learn about the process of adding products to your store here.

* The actual adding of products section. It is the place where you add items to your store once you've completed the instruction and have a thorough knowledge of the procedure.

Introduction to Add Products

To include a product in your online store, you should be prepared with a few items including the item itself as well as an image for the item to include on the listing, and an understanding of the exact stock of the item. There are four fundamental steps to add products to your store.

1. Add the title. It's the same procedure as making the post on Wordpress.

2. Add images. You can upload several.

3. The description should be added. The description provides the buyer with an in-depth understanding of the purpose of the product and its worth.

4. It is possible to organize the items by shape, color and size. So that anyone seeking a product that has specific qualities can locate it quickly.

Add Your First Product Listing

The process of adding your first item from an admin panel, that is quickly located by clicking on the Products hyperlink on the home page. On the page, you'll see an option titled "Add Product. When you click that, you will be directed to a page that has the option to add a to a new page.'

Below, you'll complete the following form:

* Title. If, for instance, you owned a company selling purple socks the first entry could be plain pink socks.'

* Description. For instance, "These high quality, comfortable socks are ideal for all

lovers of purple and they are one size will fit all."

* Image(s). Make sure you include an image description too in the event that the image doesn't load on the device of someone else.

* Organization. The next step is to classify the particular item to a particular area of your shop. For example, if , for instance, you sell socks in purple with various designs This particular item could fall in"plain" or the "plain" category Other possible categories including "patterns," "animals" and "pop culture".

* Price. This is where you decide on the price you would like to sell the item for sale at. It is possible to look at it in comparison to your "original" price as well as the price you are selling it at is what you're selling it at "now." It doesn't necessarily need to have been able to get a better "original" price for the product. This creates the appearance of bargains, since your customers may think that they're receiving the product at a cheaper price.

Controlling a variety of Listings

"The Search" Tool. It is located at the bottom of the sidebar this tool allows you to include product descriptions to specific collections so that customers are able to quickly find what they're looking for simply by searching it in your website.

• Inventory tracking. The inventory tracking number you have is you Stock Keeping Unit (SKU) as well as your barcode. (If you're selling books, the former is known as"the International Standard Book Number [ISBNISBN.)

• Shipping information. This section will provide details about the weight of a product when shipping, as well the applicable tariff code for international trade.

* Variants. If you have products that aren't typical for your store, you'll be listing variant features such as size, color, etc. -- as well as a different price.

The SEO preview is available. This allows you to see your HTML versions of your page and lets you have access to SEO settings for your site.

Transfer of Products

Shopify helps you track the incoming inventory easy. You can enable this feature by visiting the Add Product page' and then clicking the option to edit under the section titled Variants. The button you're searching for from this page is "Shopify is able to track the inventory of this item". The transfer of your products are tracked by Shopify. When you purchase a transfer it is necessary to keep track of the inventory that you received from the supplier you bought from. In the transfer page the user clicks "Add Transfer" and select the appropriate supplier (or make a new selection). Select the quantity you need and save. The date of delivery can be located in this section, and you will be able to monitor the progress of your order on Shopify's website until it arrives at the address. When it arrives arrive, you'll be able accept or decline the delivery. It is also possible to set up gifts cards for your customers on this page.

Setup of Shipping

If you're not thinking of being an individual business that handles all shipping by yourself the first of your duties will be to develop shipping policies and determine which firm you'll use to deliver your products for you. Below are some of the specific aspects of shipping you need to think about and established prior to preparing to launch your online store.

Shipping Options

When customers check out, it's recommended to provide multiple shipping options. There are a few customers who prefer paying higher prices for a shorter delivery time. It is generally the case that offering an improved service at more money is a great idea since it's likely to include at the very least customers willing to pay the extra money and that means more chances to put more money into your pockets. The shipping options available to customers can differ depending on what is most effective for the particular item and the people who buy these products. In general there are four main shipping options that you can provide for your business.

* Manual Shipping. This option allows you to have the ability to decide on the rates for shipping of a product and select the shipping service you wish to offer. It is possible to offer customers pickup, where customers come to your store instead of sending it to them in lieu of sending. The advantage of this approach is that it allows you to hike up the cost to compensate for any other expenses incurred by you when shipping.

In the case of something weighs more than you expected, however you don't have a manual method of shipping, you could be able to cover the shipping costs yourself. However, this can result in your shipping costs being higher than the other businesses and you could lose the status of a retailer that has competitive pricing. The most ideal scenario to consider this method is when you need special handling charges for specific products, and all product is approximately the same weight and size. You can set your shipping price to be fixed regardless of the product or product, or charge a handling or delivery cost if you are selling locally.

* Shopify USPS Shipping. This is the most common Shopify way of shipping. This is the most suitable option for you if offer products that are of different sizes and weights. In addition, as Shopify's preferred delivery method, this option offers lower shipping costs and a simple integration to your store. The only thing you have to do is fill with the weight and dimensions of your item. If you've done any selling on Ebay you'll see that it's the same procedure on Shopify. The most significant benefit for your customers is that the shipping costs are clearly displayed and are available to them during checkout. They'll be presented with a variety of optionsand can select the one that is most suitable for them depending on the urgency and how much they're willing to pay. The benefit to you is a discount on the cost of shipping your items out.

* Shipping API provided from the Carrier. There are a variety of shipping companies that can offer you an Shipping Application Programming Interface (API) for example, such as FexEx or UPS. This allows you to calculate shipping costs on your own. This will save you money by making sure you don't pay

more than you need, however, you must purchase the Unlimited plan to make use of it in conjunction with Shopify.

* Dropshipping. Like we've mentioned before it is the process of selling products through an outside party, who provides the goods and without having to interact directly with them. This is a great option since it doesn't require you to go through the hassles of shipping on your own, but you'll need to pay for whatever your provider charges you for dropshipping. Another advantage dropping shipping is the fact that it allows you the possibility of offering items to customers who receive "free" shipping since your prices will be determined by the amount your supplier will charge you.

Remember that the package you select can affect the amount you can save on shipping costs with Shopify. Shipping costs are decreased the more expensive the package you select. For the Basic package, you pay $29 per month, and receive an additional 50% off shipping labels. The Pro package for $79 per month provides an additional 55% discount on shipping labels, while the Unlimited plan at

$179 gives you a 60 discount on shipping labels. Take into consideration the price you're willing pay for shipping when selecting the Shopify package.

Configuring Your Shipping Options

It is possible to access the entire range of shipping options from the 'Settings' menu and then click on the heading 'Shipping'. Below are step-by step directions and suggestions to assist you with how to adjust your settings to suit what works most effectively for you.

1. Return address. The default return address information that Shopify provides that they provide to customers is your name you choose to your shop (which may or remain in place, particularly when you're only starting out and haven't given it enough thought) and your registered address and telephone number. Remember that if you begin to ship out items, the information will be viewed by customers. So should you provide Shopify details that aren't up-to-date or a name for your store that you do not want to keep ensure that you change all of it prior to ordering shipping labels. You can edit or

delete your personal information by clicking
on the link "EDIT ADDRESS. In addition, you
can enter new information.

2. Manual Shipping. If you decide that a
manual shopping option is the best for your
online store You can enable it in the "Shipping
Zones section of the Shipping Options. Two
options to select between for shipping -- the
domestic (meaning that you can ship within
the own country) and shipping outside the
country. If you are shipping domestically, you
can modify your zones of shipping to be
limited to specific states. As we mentioned
earlier you are also able to set your normal
and heavy shipping charges at whatever you
wish for them to be. When international
shipping, you have some flexibility when it
comes to setting your rates, however it's still
limited to other alternatives.

3. Carrier Calculated Shipping. When you
purchase Unlimited parcels, you get access to
the carrier's calculate shipping and find out
the most competitive shipping rates directly
to the shipping company.

4. Shopify Shipping & Labels. There are two items to consider prior to selling products if you choose to use Shopify's shipping label for your shop. First, you must have a printer that is ready for printing the label. This can't be any printer, since Shopify labels can only be printed out on certain kinds of. The next step is to enter the specific characteristics of your product like price, which will be presented to the customer.

5. Dropshipping. If you opt to utilize dropshippers to ship your items to buyers they will require you to link them up with Shopify. Shopify can automatically connect to Shipwire, Rakuten and Amazon dropshipping, however you can create your own dropshipper connection. This is accomplished via email, where you specify where the customer's details should be sent when an order is made to ensure that orders be sent directly to the dropshipper. You are not required to act as an intermediary.

Taxes & Transaction Options Setup

To determine the way your customers make purchases go to your payment page. You will be able to connect to various options for payment and you can select the one(s) you'll provide for your shop according to your requirements and preferences. Similar to delivery, Shopify offers its very unique payment method that has fees that are different according to the payment method you select. There are other alternatives that aren't exclusive for Shopify but are included in the platform to make use of already. In this chapter , you'll be able to learn about the different options available and how to select the best one for your needs.

Making use of Shopify Payments

Shopify Payments are Shopify's own payment option. It's easy to use, but it's only available for use in four nations that include that is the United States, the United Kingdom, Australia and Canada. If you are operating in these four countries, it's an ideal choice for you. It's with a fully integrated system that can be used within your store, with minimal work from you and includes useful features, such as an extensive list of credit card optionsincluding American Express, Visa and MasterCard credit and debit cards. If you're located on the U.S.

you can even accept Diner's Club, JCB and Discover cards. You don't need to pay any charges for the transaction gateway, since Shopify is only charged the charges for the package you have purchased.

If you decide Shopify Payments are the best choice for you There are a few items you should be aware of. Two security safeguards that you can pick to guard against fraud.

The CVV is the verification. It is the three-digit number that appears on the reverse on the back of your card.

• Address verification. This is necessary to verify the zip code to which a package is delivered to match that of the address on the debit or credit card when the purchase was completed.

You are free to toggle these security features off and on, however you risk making fraud if you opt to not turn these security measures off.

Conclusion

Today multi-channel selling is popular, which entails making a sale across multiple platforms. Do not just wait for the customers to visit your website, rather attract them using platforms such as Facebook, Twitter, and Instagram. You should not be ignorant of such trends because they play an important role in connecting you with customers.

Also, you are encouraged to do a proper assessment when seeking to set up a successful Shopify store. This is where you identify a market niche. You need to identify the products that you will be dealing with   , which are those you know have a broad market and ensure customers will be willing and able to buy them online.

For instance, health and fitness products have gained significant popularity in the market. It is common to come across blogs encouraging people to be attentive with what they are eating and to exercise regularly. This increased awareness of health issues has created a market for health and fitness products. Also, there is a growing market for consumer electronics such as personal computers, laptops, smartphones, and TVs, among others. Furthermore, Millennials have created a broad market for beauty and fashion products. You should take advantage of these markets and target certain customers, provide suitable content, and give people offers that will attract them to your store.

You have been provided with an extensive discussion on how to find reliable suppliers. It has been noted that not all businesses you come across will be legitimate wholesalers, you must take your time in researching for suitable suppliers.

An aspect that you be aware of is ensuring you are selling your products at as low a price as possible. To ensure you are dealing with competitive prices and making profits at the same time, you will need to look for legitimate wholesalers or suppliers who will give you suitable market prices. From there you will be able to sell at a mark-up price.

Be cautious of the retailers who pretend to be wholesalers. They will be selling their products at a higher cost than wholesalers. When you engage with such suppliers, you will end up selling at higher prices than the competitors.

Another aspect you must compare is local and international suppliers. For instance, cost, quality, and the customers' social class will determine whether to deal with a local or international supplier. You can also come across ideal suppliers through referral, Google search, attending trade shows, or contacting manufacturers.

As noted, you need a marketing plan to succeed in differentiating your brand. A marketing plan is important because it enables you to carry out calculated and assessed actions.

When you engage in marketing planning, you get the opportunity to think and become more conversant with aspects relating to the target customers. Look at the marketing plan as a strategic plan that informs you of customer needs and wants. Also, you get to learn how to attract them, reach them, and tell them what they want to hear. It will then be possible to engage them, follow up, and convert them into customers, which in turn will increase your sales.

Related is the aspect of increasing your sales funnel through Facebook marketing. You were guided on how to reach maximum customer value. If you attain this, it means you have managed to attain a class of loyal customers and you can retain your customers.

www.ingramcontent.com/pod-product-compliance
Lightning Source LLC
Chambersburg PA
CBHW071222210326
41597CB00016B/1913